**an earth and space science unit for high-ability learners in kindergarten and first grade**

# How the
# Sun Makes
# Our Day

an earth and space science unit for high-ability learners in kindergarten and first grade

# How the
# Sun Makes
# Our Day

Project Clarion Primary Science Units
Funded by the Jacob K. Javits Program, United States Department of Education

The College of William and Mary
School of Education
Center for Gifted Education
P.O. Box 8795
Williamsburg, VA 23187-8795

Co-Principal Investigators: Bruce A. Bracken & Joyce VanTassel-Baska
Project Directors: Lori C. Bland, Tamra Stambaugh, & Valerie Gregory
Unit Developers: Elizabeth Crawford, Valerie Gregory, & Elizabeth Sutton
Unit Editors: Lori C. Bland & Cristina Reintjes

Edited by Lacy Compton
Production Design by Marjorie Parker

ISBN-13: 978-1-59363-392-9

Prufrock Press Inc.
P.O. Box 8813
Waco, TX 76714-8813
Phone: (800) 998-2208
Fax: (800) 240-0333
http://www.prufrock.com

# Contents

# Part I: Unit Overview

# Introduction to the Clarion Units

The Project Clarion Science Units for Primary Grades introduce young students to science concepts, science reasoning, and scientific investigation processes. Macroconcepts, such as systems or change, help students connect understanding of science content and processes. The units use a hands-on, constructivist approach that allows children to build their knowledge base and their skills as they explore science topics through play and planned investigations. Students are engaged in creative and critical thinking, problem finding and solving, process skill development, and communication opportunities. Conceptual understanding is reinforced as units strengthen basic language and mathematical concepts, including quantity, direction, position, comparison, colors, letter identification, numbers, counting, size, social awareness, texture, material, shape, time, and sequence.

## Introduction to the *How the Sun Makes Our Day* Unit

*How the Sun Makes Our Day*, a kindergarten and first-grade Earth and space science unit, engages students in investigations and observations that support their learning about the sun as a source of light and energy, the nature of shadows, and the need for humans to conserve natural resources. Students explore natural and manmade sources of energy and develop a conservation plan for their home, school, or community. Focusing on the macroconcept of change, the *How the Sun Makes Our Day* unit deepens students' understanding of the scientific concepts in the unit.

## Curriculum Framework

The curriculum framework (see Table 1) developed for the Project Clarion science units is based on the Integrated Curriculum Model (ICM), which posits the relatively equal importance of teaching to high-level content, higher order processes and resultant products, and important concepts and issues. The model represents a research-based set of differentiated curricular and instructional approaches found appropriate for high-ability learners (VanTassel-Baska, 1986; VanTassel-Baska & Little, 2003). The framework serves several important functions:

1. The curriculum framework provides scaffolding for the central concept of change, the scientific research process, and the content of the units.
2. The curriculum framework also provides representative statements of advanced, complex, and sophisticated learner outcomes. It demonstrates how a single set of outcomes for all can be translated appropriately for high-ability learners yet can remain accessible to other learners.
3. The curriculum framework provides a way for readers to get a snapshot view of the key emphases of the curriculum in direct relation to each other. The model also provides a way to traverse the elements individually through the continuum of grade levels.

Moreover, the framework may be used to implement the William and Mary units and to aid in new curriculum development based on science reform recommendations.

# Table 1
# Project Clarion Curriculum
# Framework for Science Units

| Goal | Student Outcomes<br>The student will be able to: |
|---|---|
| 1. Develop concepts related to understanding the world of science. | • Provide examples and salient features of various concepts.<br>• Classify various concepts.<br>• Identify counterexamples of various concepts.<br>• Create definitions or generalizations about various concepts. |
| 2. Develop an understanding of the macroconcept of change as applied to science content goals. | • Provide examples of change.<br>• Articulate that change happens over time.<br>• Categorize examples of natural changes and manmade changes.<br>• Evaluate the nature of change (predictable or random) in selected phenomena. |
| 3. Develop knowledge of selected content topics in Earth and space science. | • Articulate that shadows can occur whenever light is present.<br>• Understand that shadows can be produced by blocking artificial light.<br>• Observe and measure changes associated with the sun and shadows.<br>• Investigate and identify how the sun is a natural source of heat and light.<br>• Determine how natural resources help humans.<br>• Understand that shadows occur in nature when light is blocked by an object.<br>• Conclude how night and day are caused by the rotation of the Earth.<br>• Analyze how recycling, reusing, and reducing consumption may help reduce global warming. |
| 4. Develop interrelated science process skills. | • Make observations.<br>• Ask questions.<br>• Learn more.<br>• Design and conduct the experiment.<br>• Create meaning.<br>• Tell others what was found. |
| 5. Develop critical thinking skills. | • Describe problematic situations or issues.<br>• Define relevant concepts.<br>• Identify different points of view in situations or issues.<br>• Describe evidence or data supporting a scientific question.<br>• Draw conclusions based on data (making inferences).<br>• Predict consequences. |
| 6. Develop creative thinking skills. | • Develop fluency when naming objects and ideas, based on a stimulus.<br>• Develop flexible thinking.<br>• Elaborate on ideas presented in oral or written form.<br>• Create novel products. |
| 7. Develop curiosity and interest in the world of science. | • Express reactions about discrepant events.<br>• Ask meaningful questions about science topics.<br>• Articulate ideas of interest about science.<br>• Demonstrate persistence in completing science tasks. |

## Standards Alignment

Each lesson was aligned to the appropriate National Science Education Standards (NSES), Content Standards: K–4 (Center for Science, Mathematics, and Engineering Education, CSMEE, 1996). Table 2 presents detailed information on the alignment between the NSES Content Standards and fundamental concepts within the unit lessons.

# Table 2
## *How the Sun Makes Our Day* Alignment to National Science Education Standards

| Standard | Fundamental Concepts | Unit Lesson |
|---|---|---|
| Content Standard A: Abilities necessary to do scientific inquiry | • Ask a question about objects, organisms, and events in the environment.<br>• Plan and conduct a simple investigation.<br>• Employ simple equipment and tools to gather data and extend the senses.<br>• Use data to construct a reasonable explanation.<br>• Communicate investigations and explanations. | 1, 2, 3, 4, 5, 6, 7, 8, 9, 10, 11, 12, 13 |
| Content Standard A: Understanding about scientific inquiry | • Scientific investigations involve asking and answering a question and comparing the answer with what scientists already know about the world.<br>• Scientists use different kinds of investigations depending on the questions they are trying to answer. Types of investigations include: describing objects, events, and organisms; classifying them; and doing a fair test (experimenting).<br>• Simple instruments, such as magnifiers, thermometers, and rulers, provide more information than scientists obtain using only their senses.<br>• Scientists develop explanations using observations (evidence) and what they already know about the world (scientific knowledge). Good explanations are based on evidence from investigations.<br>• Scientists make the results of their investigations public; they describe the investigation in ways that enable others to repeat the investigation.<br>• Scientists review and ask questions about the results of other scientists' work. | 1, 2, 3, 4, 5, 6, 7, 8, 9, 10, 11, 12, 13 |
| Content Standard B: Light, heat, electricity, and magnetism | • Light travels in a straight line until it strikes an object. Light can be reflected by a mirror, refracted by a lens, or absorbed by an object. | 3, 4, 13 |
| Content Standard D: Objects in the sky | • The sun, moon, stars, clouds, birds, and airplanes all have properties, locations, and movements that can be observed and described.<br>• The sun provides the light and heat necessary to maintain the temperature of the Earth. | 7, 10, 11, 12, 13 |
| Content Standard D: Changes in Earth and sky | • Objects in the sky have patterns of movement. The sun, for example, appears to move across the sky in the same way every day, but its path changes slowly over the seasons. Objects move across the sky on a daily basis much like the sun. The observable shape of the moon changes from day to day in a cycle that lasts about a month. | 7, 13 |
| Content Standard E: Understanding about science and technology | • People have always had problems and invented tools and techniques (ways of doing something) to solve problems. Trying to determine the effects of solutions helps people avoid some new problems. | 6, 11, 12, 13 |
| Content Standard E: Abilities to distinguish between natural objects and objects made by humans | • Some objects occur in nature; others have been designed and made by people to solve human problems and enhance the quality of life.<br>• Objects can be categorized into two groups: natural and designed. | 6, 8, 13 |

## Macroconcept

The macroconcept for this unit is *change*. A concept paper on change is included in Appendix A. The natural world changes continually; however, some changes may be too slow to observe. Students begin to understand the concept of change in science by learning about natural changes that occur over time, as well as manmade changes that impact conditions. The second lesson in this unit introduces the concept of change. Students are asked to brainstorm examples of change, categorize their examples, identify "nonexamples" of the concept, and make generalizations about the concept (Taba, 1962). The generalizations about change incorporated into this unit of study include:

- Change is everywhere.
- Change is related to time.
- Change can be natural or manmade.
- Change may be random or predictable.

The concept of change is integrated throughout the unit lessons and deepens students' understanding of animals and plants. Students examine the relationship of important ideas, abstractions, and issues through application of the concept generalizations. This higher-level thinking enhances the students' ability to "think like a scientist." More information about concept development is provided in Appendix B: Teaching Models.

## Key Science Concepts

By the end of this unit, students will understand that:
- Shadows can occur whenever light is present.
- Shadows can be produced when light is blocked.
- Changes in the sun and shadows can be observed and measured.
- The sun is a natural source of heat and light.
- Natural resources help humans.
- Day and night are caused by the rotation of the Earth.
- Shadows occur in nature when light is blocked by an object.
- Recycling, reusing, and reducing consumption may help to reduce global warming.

Practice in using concept maps supports students' learning as they begin to build upon known concepts (Novak & Gowin, 1984). Students begin to add new concepts to their initial understandings of a topic and to make new connections between concepts. The use of concept maps within the lessons also helps teachers to recognize students' conceptual frameworks so that instruction can be adapted as necessary. More information on strategies for using concept mapping, as well as a list of concept-mapping practice activities, is provided in Appendix B: Teaching Models.

Each Project Clarion unit contains a science concept map (see Figure 1) that displays the key science concepts and the connections students should be able to make as a result of their experiences within the unit. This overview may be useful as a classroom poster that teachers and students can refer to throughout the unit.

## Scientific Investigation and Reasoning

The Wheel of Scientific Investigation and Reasoning contains the specific processes involved in scientific inquiry that guide students' thinking and actions. To read more about these processes and suggestions for implementing the wheel into this unit's lessons, see Appendix B: Teaching Models.

The following lessons utilize the Wheel of Scientific Investigation and Reasoning:
- Lessons 1, 3, and 5, which help students gain a better understanding of what scientists do and introduce the Wheel of Scientific Investigation and Reasoning, including the six components of scientific investigation.

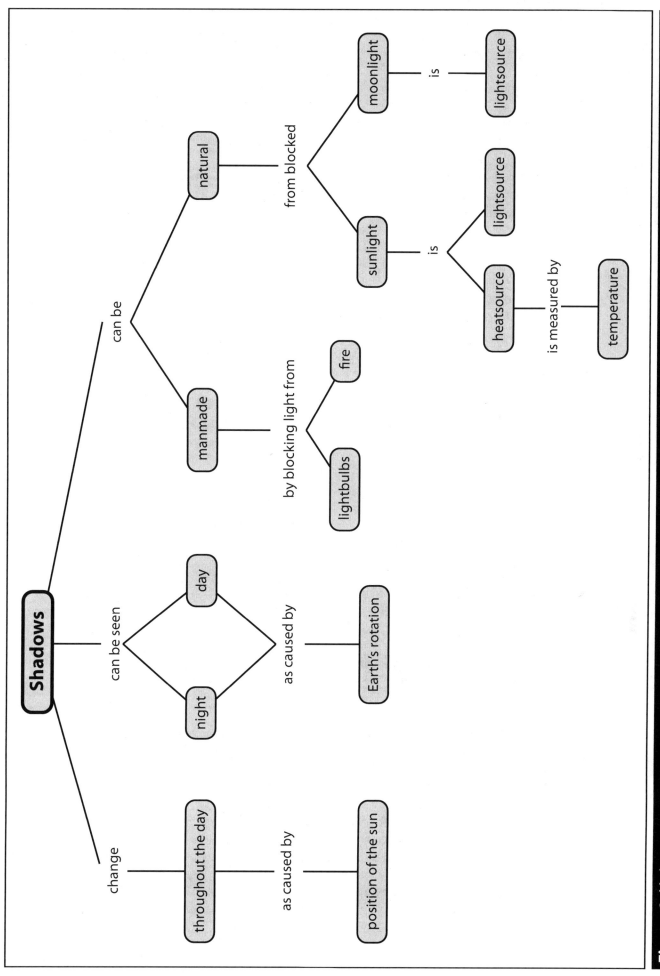

**Figure 1.** Unit concept map.

7

- Lessons 4 and 6–13, which include additional lessons on scientific investigation by requiring students to make observations, ask questions, learn more about a topic, design and conduct experiments, create meaning, or tell others what was found.

Students apply the components of scientific investigation throughout the unit and use the wheel to analyze aspects of an investigation or to plan an investigation. Scientific investigation concepts within the lessons include:
- *Make Observations:* Scientists use their senses as well as instruments to note details, identify similarities and differences, and record changes in phenomena.
- *Ask Questions:* Scientists use information from their observations about familiar objects or events to develop important questions that spark further investigation.
- *Learn More:* Scientists carefully review what is known about a topic and determine what additional information must be sought.
- *Design and Conduct the Experiment:* Scientists design an experiment, which is a fair test of a hypothesis or prediction and is intended to answer a question for a scientific investigation.
- *Create Meaning:* Scientists carefully gather and record data from an experiment, then analyze the data.
- *Tell Others What Was Found:* Scientists communicate findings from an experiment, including a clear description of the question, the hypothesis or prediction, the experiment that was conducted, the data that were collected and how they were analyzed, and the conclusions and inferences that were made from the experiment.

## Assessment

The unit includes performance-based assessments for students to complete at the beginning (preassessment) and end (postassessment) of the unit. There are three pre- and postassessments, which assess conceptual understanding, science content knowledge, and application of the scientific investigation process. The preassessment provides baseline data that teachers can use to adjust instructional plans for individual students or groups of students. Preteaching activities accompany selected preassessments.

The postassessment is administered at the completion of the unit and provides valuable information about students' mastery of the targeted objectives and the National Science Education Standards. A rubric is used to score each pre- and postassessment. The pre- and postassessments and dimensions of learning scored for each task include:
- *A macroconcept template, which requires students to draw or write about the macroconcept.* Conceptual understanding is scored on the pre- and postassessments based on the number of appropriate examples of the macroconcept, the elements of the macroconcept, types of the macroconcept listed, and generalizations about the macroconcept.
- *Concept maps, which assess students' content knowledge.* Students are given a prompt for creating a concept map about the unit topic. Understanding of key science concepts is scored on the pre- and postassessments based on the number of appropriate hierarchical levels, propositions, and examples listed.
- *An experimental design template, which requires students to plan an experiment with a given scientific research question.* Students are asked to design an experiment to investigate a question. Students are scored on the pre- and postassessments on their ability to write a prediction or hypothesis, list

materials needed for the experiment, list the steps of the experiment in order, and develop a plan to organize data for collection and interpretation.

Teachers also should note that assessment "Look Fors" are designated in the first section of each lesson plan. The "Look Fors" provide a means for teachers to assess student learning in each lesson. The "Look Fors" are linked to the macroconcept generalizations, key science concepts, and scientific processes identified in each lesson. Teachers can develop checklists for the "Look Fors" or may make informal observations.

# Teacher's Guide to Content

The following definitions of key science concepts taught in the unit are described along with a unit glossary and a list of content resources.

## Day and Night: Rotation of the Earth

The Earth rotates around an imaginary axis that runs through its center from the North Pole to the South Pole. It takes approximately 24 hours for the Earth to rotate around its axis one time. As the Earth rotates, different regions face the sun. The region of the globe facing the sun will experience daylight while the opposite side of the globe experiences night.

## Seasons: The Earth Revolves Around the Sun

As the Earth is rotating on its axis, it also is revolving in an elliptical orbit around the sun. It takes 365.25 days for the Earth to revolve completely around the Sun. The axis is tilted 23.5 degrees in respect to its orbit around the sun, with the North Pole pointed toward the North Star, Polaris. This tilt causes the seasons on Earth to change. As the Earth revolves around the sun, the northern and southern hemispheres lean closer to, or farther away from, the sun. As a hemisphere moves closer to the path of the sun's light and heat, it experiences summer. As it moves away from the sun, it experiences winter. Regions located on or near the Equator (the imaginary line that bisects the Earth around the middle) remain in the path of the sun all year long. As a result, these regions experience little seasonal change. They remain hot all year round. Similarly, the polar regions never spend time directly in the path of the sun's light and heat, so they experience cold temperatures throughout the year.

When designing passive solar homes in the United States, builders take into account the sun's changing position in the sky. In the winter, the sun is low in the southern sky. South-facing windows can let in the sunshine and contribute to warming the house. During summer, when the sun is high in the sky, overhangs or awnings over windows can block the sun's rays, preventing solar energy from warming the house too much.

## Shadows

Every day, the sun appears to cross the sky from east to west because of the Earth's rotation. For thousands of years, people have noticed that shadow length changes during the day. On a daily basis, the length of shadows decreases from a maximum at sunrise to a minimum at noon. From noon to sunset, the shadows become progressively longer again. A common misconception is that at noon the sun is directly overhead and there are no shadows. In fact, the sun is never directly overhead anywhere at anytime in the continental United States.

Shadows also are affected by the season. Due to the Earth's tilt and revolution around the sun, an object's shadow will get longer as you approach winter in the Northern Hemisphere if you measure it at the same time and location each day. The length of shadows increases after the summer solstice and decreases after the winter solstice. The sun is lowest in the sky in winter and highest in summer. In winter months, the sun is low in the southern sky and shadows cast will be longer than those made in the summer. After the winter solstice, the sun slowly gets higher in the southern sky and shadows cast at noon slowly get shorter until the summer solstice in June.

## Greenhouse Effect

The greenhouse effect is the rise in temperature that the Earth experiences because certain gases in the atmosphere trap energy from the sun, including water vapor, methane, carbon dioxide, nitrous oxide, and ozone. Without these gases, heat would escape back into space and Earth's average temperature would be about 60 degrees Fahrenheit colder. These gases are referred to as greenhouse gases because of how they warm our world.

The greenhouse effect is important. Without the greenhouse effect, the Earth would not be warm enough for humans to live. However, the greenhouse effect is becoming stronger as humans are causing an increase in the amount of greenhouse gasses in the atmosphere through the burning of fossil fuels, increased population, animal agriculture, and other factors. This is making the Earth warmer on average than usual. This often is referred to as global warming, also known as global climate change.

## Global Climate Change

Climate is the long-term average of a region's weather events lumped together. Climate change represents a change in these long-term weather patterns. Although some regions of the Earth are becoming colder, the net effect is one of warming. Earth has warmed by about 1.3 degrees over the past 100 years. Even a little warming may cause major problems for humans, plants, and wildlife, including greater storms and longer hurricane seasons, flooding, the loss of coastal areas due to increases in sea level, and shifts in rain patterns that may cause problems for drinking water, agriculture, and loss of habitat for wildlife.

# Unit Glossary

**Atmosphere:** the mixture of gases that surrounds a planet.

**Conservation**: the act or process of protecting forests, wildlife, and natural resources.

**Global warming**: an increase in the average temperature in the Earth's atmosphere over time.

**Greenhouse effect:** a phenomenon that takes place when gases such as carbon dioxide and methane collect in the atmosphere and prevent some of the sun's heat from escaping.

**Light:** visible electromagnetic radiation; brightness, as from the sun or a lamp.

**Light source:** place from which natural or manmade light is produced.

**Natural resources:** materials supplied by nature that are necessary or useful to people, such as forests, water, and minerals.

**Opaque:** no light is allowed through a material.

**Recycle:** to process waste materials such as glass, plastic, newspapers, and aluminum cans so that they can be used to make new products.

**Rotate:** to turn around on an axis or center.

**Shade:** an area sheltered from light.

**Shadow:** a darkened area made by something blocking out light.

**Silhouette:** an outline of an object.

**Solid:** a state of matter in which the molecules of an object are densely packed so that it retains its shape; not a liquid or gas.

**Sundial:** an instrument that indicates the time of day by using the sun's light.

**Temperature:** measures how hot or cold something is.

**Terminator:** the line between light and dark on the Earth.

**Thermometer:** an instrument for measuring temperature.

**Translucent:** some light is let through a material, but objects are not completely clear.

**Transparent:** light is let through a clear material like glass so that the other side can be seen clearly.

# Teaching Resources

## Required Resources (Used in Relevant Lessons)

Bulla, C. (1994). *What makes a shadow?* New York, NY: HarperCollins.

Dooling, M. (2005). *Young Thomas Edison.* New York, NY: Holiday House.

Ganeri, A. (2004). *Day and night.* Chicago, IL: Heinemann Library.

Lehn, B. (1999). *What is a scientist?* Minneapolis, MN: The Millbrook Press.

Pipe, J. (2005). *Light: What is a shadow?* Mankato, MN: Stargazer Books.

## Additional Resources

Asch, F. (2008). *The sun is my favorite star.* San Diego, CA: Voyager Books.

Bailey, J. (2006). *Sun up, sun down: The story of day and night.* Minneapolis, MN: Picture Window Books.

Branley, F. (2005). *Sunshine makes the seasons.* New York, NY: HarperCollins.

Branley, F. (2002). *The sun our nearest star.* New York, NY: HarperCollins.

Chrismer, M. (2008). *The sun.* New York, NY: Scholastic.

Donald, R. L. (2001). *Air pollution.* New York, NY: Scholastic.

Donald, R. L. (2001). *Recycling.* New York, NY: Scholastic.

Donald, R. L. (2001). *The ozone layer.* New York, NY: Scholastic.

Fletcher, R. (1997). *Twilight comes twice.* New York, NY: Clarion Books.

Fowler, A. (1997). *Energy from the sun.* New York, NY: Children's Press.

Ganeri, A. (2005). *Something old, something new: Recycling.* Chicago, IL: Heinemann Library.

Gibbons, G. (1987). *Sun up, sun down.* San Diego, CA: Voyager Books.

Kerrod, R. (2000). *The sun.* Minneapolis, MN: Lerner Publications.

Miller, R. (2002). *The sun.* Brookfield, CT: 21st Century Books.

Murphy, P. (2005). *Why is the sun so hot?* New York, NY: Rosen Publishing Group.

Riley, P. (2008). *Light and dark.* London, England: Franklin Watts.

Ross, M. (2001). *Earth cycles.* Minneapolis, MN: Millbrook Press.

Spangenburg, R., & Moser, K. (2001). *A look at the sun.* New York, NY: Scholastic.

Tomecek, S. (2001). *Sun.* Washington, DC: National Geographic Society.

## Useful Websites

Department of Earth Science at the University of Northern Iowa. (n.d.). *Length of shadows.* Retrieved from http://www.Earth.uni.edu/EECP/elem/mod3_matact.html

Hansen, A. (2001). *Greenhouse effect* (Flash animation). Retrieved from http://earthguide.ucsd.edu/earthguide/diagrams/greenhouse

Odenwald, S. (n.d.). *Earth—Rotation.* Retrieved from http://image.gsfc.nasa.gov/poetry/ask/arot.html

Pidwirny, M. (2009). *The greenhouse effect.* Retrieved from http://www.physicalgeography.net/fundamentals/7h.html

Sanford, W. (n.d.). *Me and my shadow: Making the sun-Earth connection.* Retrieved from http://www.wsanford.com/~wsanford/exo/sundials/shadows.html

Stanford Solar Center. (2008). *For educators.* Retrieved from http://solar-center.stanford.edu/teachers

Union of Concerned Scientists. (2010). *Global warming*. Retrieved from http://www.ucsusa.org/global_warming

United States Environmental Protection Agency. (2010). *Climate change: What it is* . . . . Retrieved from http://www.epa.gov/climatechange/kids/cc.html

World Wildlife Fund. (2008). *Solutions to global climate change*. Retrieved from http://worldwildlife.org/TOM/2005highlights/global-warming.cfm

# Part II: Lesson Plans

## Lesson Plans

Overview of Lessons

Lesson 1: What Is a Scientist?

Lesson 2: What Is Change?

Lesson 3: What Scientists Do—Observe, Question, Learn More

Lesson 4: What Is a Shadow?

Lesson 5: What Scientists Do—Experiment, Create Meaning, Tell Others

Lesson 6: Shed a Little Light on Me

Lesson 7: The Difference in Day and Night

Lesson 8: Me and My Shadow

Lesson 9: Watching Shadows Grow

Lesson 10: Temperatures in Sun and Shade

Lesson 11: The Greenhouse Effect

Lesson 12: It's Getting Hot Down Here!

Lesson 13: Shining With Shadows

Postassessment

# Overview of Lessons

An overview of the lessons is provided in Table 3. The overview shows the primary emphasis of each lesson in the unit according to the macroconcept, key science concepts, or the scientific investigation process. Lessons may also have a secondary emphasis, which is listed in the planning section of each lesson, labeled "Planning the Lesson."

# Table 3
# Overview of Lessons

| Concept of Change | Scientific Process | Key Science Concepts |
|---|---|---|
| Preassessment | | |
| | Lesson 1: What Is a Scientist? | |
| Lesson 2: What Is Change? | | |
| | Lesson 3: What Scientists Do—Observe, Question, Learn More | |
| | | Lesson 4: What Is a Shadow? |
| | Lesson 5: What Scientists Do—Experiment, Create Meaning, Tell Others | |
| | | Lesson 6: Shed a Little Light on Me |
| | | Lesson 7: The Difference in Day and Night |
| | | Lesson 8: Me and My Shadow |
| | Lesson 9: Watching Shadows Grow | |
| | Lesson 10: Temperatures in Sun and Shade | |
| | | Lesson 11: The Greenhouse Effect |
| | Lesson 12: It's Getting Hot Down Here! | |
| Lesson 13: Shining With Shadows | | |
| Postassessment | | |

## Lesson Plan Blueprint

The lesson plan blueprint (see Table 4) for each lesson shows:
- the instructional purpose,
- generalizations about the macroconcept of change,
- key science concepts,
- scientific investigation skills and processes, and
- assessment "Look Fors."

# Table 4
# Lesson Plan Blueprint

| Lesson # | Title | Instructional Purpose | Macroconcept Generalizations | Key Science Concepts | Scientific Investigation Skills and Processes | Assessment "Look Fors" Students should be able to: |
|---|---|---|---|---|---|---|
| | Preassessment | | | | | |
| 1 | What Is a Scientist? | • To learn the characteristics of scientists and the investigation skills that scientists use. | | | • Make observations.<br>• Ask questions.<br>• Learn more.<br>• Design and conduct the experiment.<br>• Create meaning.<br>• Tell others what was found. | • Identify the scientific investigation processes used by scientists. |
| 2 | What Is Change? | • To understand the concept of change.<br>• To learn four generalizations about change that will deepen understanding of the sun, shadows, and conservation. | • Change is everywhere.<br>• Change is related to time.<br>• Change can be natural or manmade.<br>• Change may be random or predictable. | | • Make observations. | • Give examples of things that change.<br>• Give examples of things that don't change.<br>• Apply change generalizations.<br>• Use size, comparison, and time/sequence concepts to describe change. |
| 3 | What Scientists Do—Observe, Question, Learn More | • To learn about the Wheel of Scientific Investigation and Reasoning.<br>• To apply three of six investigation processes (make observations, ask questions, and learn more) to investigate how shadows are produced. | • Change can be natural or manmade. | • Shadows can occur whenever light is present.<br>• Shadows can be produced when light is blocked. | • Make observations.<br>• Ask questions.<br>• Learn more.<br>• Design and conduct the experiment.<br>• Create meaning.<br>• Tell others what was found. | • Use size, comparison, and time/sequence concepts to describe observations.<br>• Apply the scientific investigation processes.<br>• Understand how shadows are produced. |
| 4 | What Is a Shadow? | • To investigate how shadows occur.<br>• To analyze how shadows change as the direction of the light source changes. | • Change is related to time.<br>• Change can be natural or manmade. | • Shadows can occur whenever light is present.<br>• Shadows can be produced when light is blocked.<br>• Changes in the sun and shadows can be observed and measured. | • Make observations.<br>• Learn more. | • Describe and explain how shadows are produced.<br>• Describe and analyze how shadows can change due to the direction of the light source.<br>• Use comparison and direction/position concepts to describe shadows. |

*Table 4, continued*

| Lesson # | Title | Instructional Purpose | Macroconcept Generalizations | Key Science Concepts | Scientific Investigation Skills and Processes | Assessment "Look Fors" Students should be able to: |
|---|---|---|---|---|---|---|
| 5 | What Scientists Do—Experiment, Create Meaning, Tell Others | • To apply the Wheel of Scientific Investigation and Reasoning to design and conduct an experiment about how shadows are produced, to create meaning from the experiment, and to tell others what was found. | • Change is everywhere.<br>• Change is related to time.<br>• Change can be natural or manmade.<br>• Change may be random or predictable. | • Shadows can be produced when light is blocked.<br>• Shadows can occur whenever light is present.<br>• Changes in the sun and shadows can be observed and measured. | • Design and conduct the experiment.<br>• Create meaning.<br>• Tell others what was found. | • Use size, comparison, and time/sequence concepts to describe observations.<br>• Apply the steps of scientific investigation.<br>• Interpret data from a data table.<br>• Describe how the experiment was conducted and what results were found.<br>• Understand how shadows are produced. |
| 6 | Shed a Little Light on Me | • To distinguish between natural and manmade sources of light.<br>• To understand how scientific investigation leads to discoveries or inventions that improve our world, such as the light bulb, a manmade light source invented by Thomas Edison. | • Change can be natural or manmade.<br>• Change may be random or predictable. | • Shadows can be produced by blocking light.<br>• The sun is a natural source of heat and light.<br>• Natural resources help humans. | • Ask questions. | • Sequence the progression from natural to manmade light sources.<br>• Identify and explain sources of light that produce shadows.<br>• Explain how change was created with the invention of the light bulb.<br>• Describe how scientific investigation helps to improve the quality of our lives. |
| 7 | The Difference in Day and Night | • To understand that the Earth's rotation causes the appearance of day and night.<br>• To apply the change concept to examine how time is related to the movement of the Earth. | • Change is related to time. | • Changes in the sun and shadows can be observed and measured.<br>• Day and night are caused by the rotation of the Earth. | • Learn more. | • Demonstrate the Earth's counterclockwise rotation on its axis.<br>• Understand that day and night are caused by the Earth's rotation on its axis.<br>• Analyze how time is related to the movement of the Earth and day and night. |
| 8 | Me and My Shadow | • To continue to explore the nature of shadows and the sun by making observations, asking questions, and learning more to investigate how long and short shadows are produced by the sun's position in the sky. | • Change is everywhere.<br>• Change can be natural or manmade.<br>• Change may be random or predictable. | • Shadows can occur whenever light is present.<br>• Shadows occur in nature when light is blocked by an object.<br>• Changes in the sun and shadows can be observed and measured. | • Make observations.<br>• Ask questions.<br>• Learn more. | • Describe and analyze how shadows can change based on the direction of the light source.<br>• Relate observed changes in shadows to generalizations about change.<br>• Use size, comparison, shape, and direction/position concepts to describe and analyze how shadows change. |
| 9 | Watching Shadows Grow | • To design and conduct an experiment to investigate how the sun's direction at various times of the day affects the size and shape of shadows. | • Change is related to time. | • Shadows can occur whenever light is present.<br>• Shadows occur in nature when light is blocked by an object. | • Design and conduct the experiment.<br>• Create meaning.<br>• Tell others what was found. | • Relate the direction and position of the sun to shadow length.<br>• Compare and contrast shadow lengths throughout the day.<br>• Describe how time creates changes in shadows.<br>• Use direction/position and time/sequence concepts to analyze and describe changes in shadows.<br>• Design and conduct an experiment.<br>• Interpret experiment findings and tell others. |

| Lesson # | Title | Instructional Purpose | Macroconcept Generalizations | Key Science Concepts | Scientific Investigation Skills and Processes | Assessment "Look Fors" Students should be able to: |
|---|---|---|---|---|---|---|
| 10 | Temperatures in Sun and Shade | • To design an experiment to investigate temperatures in sunny and shady locations to better understand the sun as a source of heat. | • Change can be natural or manmade.<br>• Change may be random or predictable. | • The sun is a natural source of heat and light. | • Design and conduct the experiment.<br>• Create meaning.<br>• Tell others what was found. | • Design and apply steps to conduct an experiment.<br>• Interpret data from a data table.<br>• Determine how shadows influence air temperature. |
| 11 | The Greenhouse Effect | • To investigate the greenhouse effect that is produced by the sun and the Earth's atmosphere.<br>• To understand how the greenhouse effect helps to keep people warm. | • Change can be natural or manmade. | • The sun is a natural source of heat and light.<br>• Natural resources help humans. | • Make observations.<br>• Design and conduct the experiment.<br>• Create meaning.<br>• Tell others what was found. | • Describe how the greenhouse effect is produced by the sun.<br>• Determine how the greenhouse effect helps to keep us warm.<br>• Investigate and observe differences in temperatures in a simulation of the greenhouse effect.<br>• Use comparison, quantity, and time/sequence concepts to make observations.<br>• Identify the steps of scientific investigation. |
| 12 | It's Getting Hot Down Here! | • To analyze how human activity causes an increase in the Earth's temperature (global warming).<br>• To identify ways to decrease factors that contribute to global warming. | • Change is everywhere.<br>• Change is related to time.<br>• Change can be natural or manmade.<br>• Change may be random or predictable. | • Recycling, reusing, and reducing consumption may help to reduce global warming. | | • Identify causes of global warming.<br>• Identify ways to help reduce global warming. |
| 13 | Shining With Shadows | • To celebrate what has been learned about the sun and shadows, change, and scientific investigation by creating shadow figures using manmade and natural light sources. | • Change is everywhere.<br>• Change is related to time.<br>• Change can be natural or manmade.<br>• Change may be random or predictable. | • Shadows can occur whenever light is present.<br>• Shadows can be produced when light is blocked.<br>• Changes in the sun and shadows can be observed and measured.<br>• The sun is a natural source of heat and light.<br>• Natural resources help humans.<br>• Shadows occur in nature when light is blocked by an object.<br>• Day and night are caused by the rotation of the Earth.<br>• Recycling, reusing, and reducing consumption may help to reduce global warming. | • Make observations.<br>• Ask questions.<br>• Learn more.<br>• Design and conduct an experiment.<br>• Create meaning.<br>• Tell others what was found. | • Apply the change generalizations to review their study of the sun, shadows, and conservation.<br>• Apply knowledge of shadows to create and change shadow figures.<br>• Distinguish between natural and manmade light sources.<br>• Hypothesize about or predict shadows.<br>• Describe the process of scientific investigation. |

# Preteaching Lesson: Science Safety

## Planning the Lesson

### Instructional Purpose

- To instill in students the importance of safety in the classroom.
- To outline science safety rules to be implemented throughout the unit.

### Instructional Time
- 45 minutes

### Materials/Resources/Equipment
- Sample materials:
  - Plant
  - Plastic bag of nonhazardous powdery substance (e.g., sugar)
  - Closed jar of nonhazardous liquid (e.g., water)

- Plastic disposable gloves
- Safety goggles
- Chart paper
- Markers
- Science Safety Guidelines (Handout 0A)
- Science Safety Rules printed on chart paper (Handout 0B)

## Implementing the Lesson

1. Display sample materials on a long table in front of students. Inform students that they soon will begin a science unit in which they will observe and study many different kinds of materials, such as these. Explain that it is important for students to practice safety during the investigations. Relate the necessity of science safety rules to those of the classroom and in physical education.
2. Display and define each item. Tell students that as a class they will create a list of rules they should follow when handling these materials. Have students think about how they can keep their bodies safe. Record these examples on chart paper.
3. Next, unveil the Science Safety Rules (Handout 0A) on chart paper. Have students compare the two lists. How do students' examples relate to these rules? If necessary, add additional rules to the list.
4. Explain why some materials (such as knives) or elements (such as fire) are never appropriate for children to handle in school. Briefly discuss the potential hazards associated with these materials.
5. Finally, conduct a brief demonstration to illustrate how to practice safety guidelines. Take the plastic bag containing a nonhazardous powdery substance and the jar of nonhazardous liquid. Explain that you are going to investigate how the two materials interact. Ask students how you can be safe while doing this investigation. Reinforce that substances can be harmful to the eyes or skin and that they should **never** be ingested. Explain that the same is

true of plants, which can be toxic to humans. Emphasize that students should follow similar guidelines when studying plants in other science units.

6. Following students' examples of safety measures, demonstrate how to use safety goggles to protect the eyes, plastic gloves to protect the hands, and other relevant protective measures, such as pulling long hair back and wearing appropriate clothing. Conduct the demonstration by carefully pouring the powdery substance into the jar of liquid. Emphasize that you should never touch your face or mouth (and especially should not eat or drink) during science experiments.

7. Tell students that materials will be disposed of properly by the teacher after the investigation is completed. Students should not touch any potentially harmful substances.

8. Demonstrate the final rule, "Wash your hands," by properly removing the gloves (without the outside of the gloves ever touching the body) and the goggles. If there is a sink in the classroom, demonstrate how to properly wash one's hands. If no sink is present, inform students that after each investigation the class will go to the bathroom to wash their hands.

9. Conclude the lesson by emphasizing that science investigations are interesting and fun, but they also can be dangerous if not conducted properly. By following the Science Safety Rules, the class will enjoy the benefits of learning about science.

# Handout 0A
# Science Safety Guidelines

1. Know and follow your school's policies and procedures regarding classroom safety.

2. Always provide direct adult supervision when students are engaging in scientific experimentation.

3. Ensure that all materials and equipment are safe for handling by primary students.

4. Exert extra caution when materials have the potential for harm when used improperly.

5. Use protective gear for eyes, skin, and breathing when conducting experiments, and require students to do the same.

6. Always conduct an experiment by yourself before completing it with the students.

7. Store materials for experiments out of the reach of students.

8. Never allow students to eat or drink during science experiments.

9. Follow general safety rules for sharp objects, heated items, breakables, or spilled liquids.

10. Teach students that it is unsafe to touch their face, mouth, eyes, or other body parts when they are working with plants, animals, microorganisms, or chemicals. Wash hands prior to touching anything. Caution students about putting anything in their mouth or breathing in the smell of substances.

11. Be aware of students' allergies to plants (including plant pollen) animals, foods, chemicals, or other substances to be used in the science classroom. Take all precautions necessary. Common food allergens include peanuts, tree nuts (cashews, almonds, walnuts, hazelnuts, macadamia nuts, pecans, pistachios, and pine nuts), shellfish, fish, milk, eggs, wheat, and soy.

12. Use caution with plants. Never allow students to pick or handle any unknown plants, leaves, flowers, seeds, or berries. Use gloves to touch unknown plants. Many common house, garden, and wooded area plants are toxic.

13. Avoid glass jars and containers. Use plastic, paper, or cloth containers.

14. Thermometers should be filled with alcohol, not mercury.

15. Clearly label any chemicals used and dispose of properly.

16. Teach students safety rules for science (see Handout 0B), including:
    a. **Always** do scientific experiments with an adult present.
    b. **Never** mix things together (liquids, powders) without adult approval.
    c. **Use** your senses carefully. Protect your eyes, ears, nose, mouth, and skin.
    d. **Wash your hands** after using materials for an experiment.

# Science Safety Rules

**1** **Always** do scientific experiments with an adult present.

**2** **Never** mix things together (liquids, powders) without adult approval.

**3** **Use** your senses carefully. Protect your eyes, ears, nose, mouth, and skin.

**4** **Wash your hands** after using materials for an experiment.

# Preassessment

## Planning the Lesson

### Instructional Purpose
- To determine prior knowledge of unit content.
- To build understanding of the unit macroconcept, key science concepts, and science processes.

### Instructional Time
- Macroconcept assessment: 20 minutes
- Key science concepts assessment: 30 minutes, including preteaching activity
- Scientific process assessment: 20 minutes

### Materials/Resources/Equipment
- Copies of Preassessment for Change Concept, Word Bank for Animals Concept Map, and Incomplete Animals Concept Map for each student
- Preassessment for Key Science Concepts, Rubric 1 (Scoring Rubric for Change Concept), Preteaching for Key Science Concepts Preassessment, Sample Concept Map, Rubric 2 (Scoring Rubric for Content Assessment), and Rubric 3 (Scoring Rubric for Scientific Process) for your use
- Copies of Does Sand Dissolve in Water?, What Materials Will You Need?, How Would You Conduct Your Experiment?, What Does This Table Show?, and What Will Dissolve? handouts for the Preassessment for the Science Process for each student
- Pencils
- Large chart paper
- Drawing paper for each student

## Implementing the Lesson

1. Each assessment should be administered on a different day.
2. Explain to students that the class is beginning a new unit of study. Tell them that they will be completing a preassessment to determine what they already know about the topic. Assure them that the assessment is not for a grade and encourage them to do their best.
3. Collect all of the preassessments. Briefly review each assessment and discuss some of the responses in general, indicating that this unit will provide them with more knowledge and skills than they now have.

## Scoring
- Score the preassessments using the rubrics provided. Keep the scores and assessments for diagnostic purposes to organize groups for various activities during the unit and to compare pre- and postassessment results.

Name:_____ Date:_____

# Preassessment for Change Concept

1. What is change? In each box, draw a picture or write a word for something that changes.

| | |
|---|---|
| | |
| | |
| | |
| | |
| | |

2. Draw a picture of something in your life that changes and show how it changes. Include as many details as you can.

3. Draw five ways a tree could change or be changed.

Name: _____ Date: _____

# Rubric 1

# Scoring Rubric for Change Concept

**Directions for Use:** Score students on their responses to each of the questions.

|   |   | 5 | 4 | 3 | 2 | 1 | 0 |
|---|---|---|---|---|---|---|---|
| 1 | **Examples of the Concept** | At least 9–10 appropriate examples are given. | At least 7–8 appropriate examples are given. | At least 5–6 appropriate examples are given. | At least 3–4 appropriate examples are given. | At least 1–2 appropriate examples are given. | No examples are given. |
| 2 | **Drawing of Before-After** | The drawing contains 5 picture elements that depict a before-after situation. | The drawing contains 4 picture elements that depict a before-after situation. | The drawing contains 3 picture elements that depict a before-after situation. | The drawing contains 2 picture elements that depict a before-after situation. | The drawing contains only 1 picture element that depicts a before-after situation. | The drawing contains no elements that depict a before-after situation. |
| 3 | **Types of Change** | Identifies 5 different types of change. | Identifies 4 different types of change. | Identifies 3 different types of change. | Identifies 2 different types of change. | Identifies 1 different types of change. | Identifies no type of change. |

**Total possible points: 15**

# Preteaching for Key Science Concepts Preassessment

**Directions for the Teacher:** Say the following bolded directions to students. Directions for you are not bolded.

**Sometimes we know a lot about something even before our teachers teach it in school. Sometimes we don't know very much at all, but we like to learn new things.**

**For example, what would you think about if someone asked you to tell all you know about how *farms* work? What are some of the words you would use?**

(List these on a chart.)

**What are some of the things that happen on a farm?**

(List these on a chart.)

**I am going to show you a way I might tell all I know about how farms work.**

(Begin a concept map on a large sheet of paper, using pictures and words, making simple links, and emphasizing these links.)

**Practice making your own concept map about a farm on your drawing paper. This practice activity can be done with a partner.** (Note to teacher: You may also choose to assign another familiar topic for the students to practice concept mapping.)

(Share some of the resulting concept maps, encouraging students to articulate their links.)

# Preassessment for Key Science Concepts

**Directions to the Teacher:** Read the following paragraph to the students.

Today I would like you to think about all the things you know about the sun and shadows. Think about the words you would use and the pictures you could draw to make a concept map. Think about the connections you can make. You will be drawing a concept map, just like the one you did when we discussed the farm. Look at the word bank and the concept map. You will use some of the word bank words to fill in the parts of the concept map. Some words are just extras that you won't need. Remember, a concept map is used to tell what we know and to make connections. Today's question is: "Tell me everything you know about the sun and shadows."

## For Kindergarten Students

Direct students to use the word bank to complete the assessment. Students also may use other responses that they come up with on their own. Tell students to draw a picture or write the word or letter for their responses in the appropriate blanks. Each correct response earns one point. Students may enter the word *or* just the letter corresponding to the word *or* come up with their own word.

## For First-Grade Students

Direct students to complete the assessment with appropriate words, pictures, or their own choices of words. Each correct response earns one point.

Name: _____ Date: _____

# Incomplete Shadows Concept Map

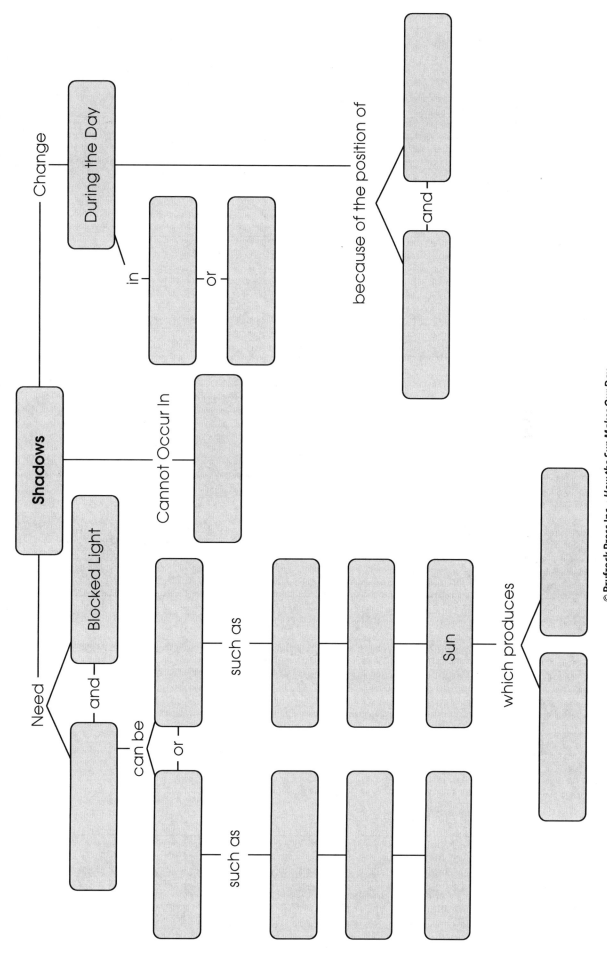

# Preassessment for Key Science Concepts
## Word Bank for Shadows Concept Map

| | | | | | | | |
|---|---|---|---|---|---|---|---|
| **Shadows need** | **A** Darkness | **B** Dust | **C** Light source | **D** Heat | **E** Shade | **F** Air | **G** Water |
| **Can be** | **H** Tomorrow | **I** Natural | **J** Black | **K** Shadow | **L** Manmade | **M** Rain | **N** Darkness |
| **Such as** | **O** Glow Stick | **P** Light bulb | **Q** Moonlight | **R** Fire | **S** Flashlight | **T** Star light | **U** Headlight |
| **Sun produces** | **V** Rain | **W** Light | **X** Cold | **Y** Heat | **Z** Pollution | **Aa** Shape | **Bb** Darkness |
| **Cannot occur in** | **Cc** Outside | **Dd** Darkness | **Ee** Winter | **Ff** Daylight | **Gg** Water | **Hh** Inside | **Ii** March |
| **Shadows change in** | **Jj** Color | **Kk** Temperature | **Ll** Shape | **Mm** Texture | **Nn** Weight | **Oo** Size | **Pp** Salt |
| **Because of the position of** | **Qq** Stars | **Rr** Moon | **Ss** Meteor | **Tt** Earth | **Uu** Sun | **Vv** Rock | **Ww** Atmosphere |

# Rubric 2
# Scoring Guide for Preassessment
# for Key Science Concepts

**Directions for Use:** Score students on their completed maps.

## Criteria

Concept Map (up to 16 points)

> Score 1 point for each correct response in the concept map. Note that the student may have chosen a word that is not in the word bank. Score 1 point as long as the word(s) complete the link accurately. Students also may receive a point for each picture that accurately completes a link.

**Total possible points: 16**

# Preassessment for the Scientific Process

1. Assess students in groups of 4 to 6.
2. Tell students they are going to think like scientists. Say to students, "I have a scientific question for you: Does sand dissolve in water? You are going to think about whether or not sand dissolves in water." We will work together to look at some pictures and select an answer to some questions about an experiment to find out if sand dissolves in water.
3. Pass out the packet of assessment record sheets on pp. 35–39. Ask students to look at the first sheet (Does Sand Dissolve in Water?). Ask them to write their name on the paper. Direct them to think about the two pictures and make a prediction about whether or not sand dissolves in water. Tell students to put an X in the box under the picture that shows their prediction—sand does not dissolve in water or sand does dissolve in water.
   Picture choices are:
   a. Clear container with water and sand on the bottom
   b. Clear container with water and no sand on the bottom

4. Ask students to think about what materials they will need for their experiment. Look at the What Materials Will You Need? handout (the one that shows some materials that could be used). Ask students to put an X under each picture that shows a material that will be used in the experiment.
   Picture choices are:
   a. Clear container
   b. Spoon
   c. Sand
   d. Salt
   e. Water
   f. Milk

5. Present each student with a set of four cards showing pictures of the steps in the experiment (see the How Would You Conduct the Experiment? handout). Tell the students to select the pictures that show the steps they would take for the experiment. Picture choices are (1) gathering the materials, (2) pouring in water, (3) pouring in sand, (4) stirring the mixture. Instruct students to put the steps they selected in the correct order—which comes first, second, etc. Check to see each student's response and record.
6. Ask students to look at the table on the What Does This Table Show? handout and decide whether it shows that sand dissolves in water or salt does not dissolve in water. Students should put an X in the correct box.
7. Ask students to look at the handout, What Will Dissolve?, with pictures of various materials. The materials are: leaf, twig, salt, JELL-O, crayon, sugar, rock, oatmeal. Direct students to think about things that probably dissolve in water and to place an X in each box under a picture that shows something that will dissolve. Which of these materials will dissolve?

Name:_____ Date:_____

# Preassessment:
# Does Sand Dissolve in Water?

Does sand dissolve in water? Put an X in the box that matches your prediction.

☐                                    ☐

# What Materials Will You Need?

What materials do you need to conduct your experiment? Put an X in the box of each material you would use.

# How Would You Conduct Your Experiment?

Cut out the pictures below and place them in order of the steps of the water and sand experiment.

Name:_____ Date:_____

# What Does This Table Show?

Did the sand dissolve in water?

| | |
|---|---|
| Cassidy | No |
| Lowell | No |
| Sandy | No |
| Adrian | No |
| Leslie | No |
| Lincoln | No |
| Jonah | No |
| Chwee | No |
| Sun | No |

___ Yes, the sand
dissolved in water.

___ No, the sand did
not dissolve in water.

Name:_____ Date:_____

# What Will Dissolve?

Put an X in the box below each picture that shows something that will dissolve in water.

☐

☐

☐

☐

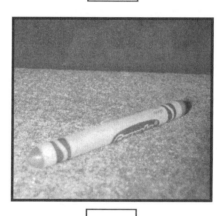

☐

☐

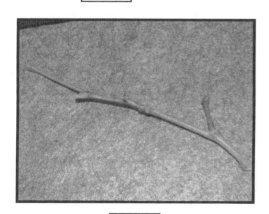

☐

☐

Name:_____ Date:_____

# Rubric 3
# Scoring Guide for Preassessment
# for Scientific Process

**Directions for Use:** Score students on the responses to each of the questions.

| Criteria | Scoring Guide | Points Available |
|---|---|---|
| Selects a prediction: Does sand dissolve in water? | Score the two glasses of water/sand as being either correct or incorrect. Give 1 point if the student selects the glass with sand at the bottom. | 1 point |
| Selects materials needed. | A total of up to 6 points is earned for checking the sand, empty glass, spoon, and water, and not checking salt or milk. | up to 6 points |
| Sequences steps. | One point is earned for each picture in its appropriate order. A total of up to 4 points may be given. The following order is correct: (1) the girl sitting with the ingredients in front of her, (2) the girl pouring water, (3) the girl pouring sand, and (4) the girl mixing. | up to 4 points |
| Selects the appropriate interpretation of the data table provided. | Two points awarded for the "No" response. | 2 points |
| Selects a prediction: What will dissolve? | One point should be given for each of the boxes being checked or not checked accurately. Checks should appear for salt, JELL-O, and sugar. No checks should appear for the remaining items. Students earn three points for each box they check correctly. | up to 9 points |

**Total possible points: _____/22**

# Lesson 1: What Is a Scientist?

## Planning the Lesson

### Instructional Purpose
- To learn the characteristics of scientists and the investigation skills that scientists use.

### Instructional Time
- 45 minutes

### Scientific Investigation Skills and Processes
- Make observations.
- Ask questions.
- Learn more.
- Design and conduct the experiment.
- Create meaning.
- Tell others what was found.

### Assessment "Look Fors"
- Students should be able to identify the scientific investigation processes used by scientists.

### Materials/Resources/Equipment
- Lab coat for teacher
- One lab coat (white adult T-shirt or dress shirt) for each student
- Beaker
- Microscope or magnifying glass
- Prepared charts for students, PowerPoint slides, or transparencies of Handout 1A (Defining Scientists) and 1B (What Scientists Do: The Wheel of Scientific Investigation and Reasoning)
- Poster of the Wheel of Scientific Investigation and Reasoning
- Marker
- One piece of chart paper
- Student log books
- *What Is a Scientist?* by Barbara Lehn

> **Note to Teacher:** Scientific investigation is introduced to the students in this lesson and applied throughout the unit.

## Implementing the Lesson

1. Put on a lab coat and pick up a beaker and microscope or magnifying glass. Ask the students what kind of job you might have. Explain that you are a scientist. Ask the students if they know a scientist and allow them to discuss what they know about scientists or their experiences with scientists. Record student responses to the following questions (you may wish to refer to the Frayer Model of Vocabulary Development in Appendix B):
   - Do you know a scientist?
   - What do you think scientists do?

2. Define a scientist as "a person who studies nature and the physical world by testing, experimenting, and measuring" (Scholastic, 2007) using Handout 1A.
3. Ask the students what they think scientists do and write down their responses on chart paper. Display the chart "What Scientists Do" (Handout 1B). Read the wheel to the students and talk about what each item means. Ask the students to compare the "What Scientists Do" processes with the list the class created.
4. Show students the book *What Is a Scientist?* by Barbara Lehn. Ask students to look for what scientists do while you are reading the book. Read the book, showing the pictures to the students and pointing out the clues that will help students understand what a scientist does. As you read each page, relate the activity to the scientific investigation processes included on the wheel. Ask students these questions:
   • What did the scientists do in the book?
   • What makes someone a scientist?
   • When is someone not a scientist?

5. Explain that the students will be working as scientists in the unit. Have students put on their "lab coats." Explain to the students that they are going to learn to think like scientists and learn how to do what scientists do.
6. Tell students that scientists keep a scientific investigation log of what they are doing. They date the pages in their logs and then write down what they have learned or what they are thinking about what they learned. Tell students that they are going to keep a log and they are going to make the first page. Pass out student log books. Ask each student to date the first page and to draw a picture of him- or herself investigating something.
7. Have students share their completed pictures with the class.

## Concluding and Extending the Lesson

### Concluding Questions and/or Actions
• Would you like to be a scientist? Why or why not?
• All science is about how things stay the same and how they change. How do scientists study change?
• Set up a learning center where students can cut pictures out of magazines, newspapers, etc., of people who are scientists and paste the pictures on a class collage.
• Provide props (e.g., magnifying glasses) and lab coats for students to practice being scientists in the science investigation center.
• Provide books on individuals who are investigating something scientific in the library center of the classroom.

### What to Do at Home
• Ask students to ask their parent or some other adult to respond to the question, "What would you investigate/do if you were a scientist?"

# Defining Scientists

## A scientist is someone who . . .

studies nature and the physical world by testing, experimenting, and measuring.
(Scholastic, 2007)

## Scientists . . .

try to find answers to questions they have about our world. Often, they improve our world by finding answers to their questions.

# What Scientists Do: The Wheel of Scientific Investigation and Reasoning

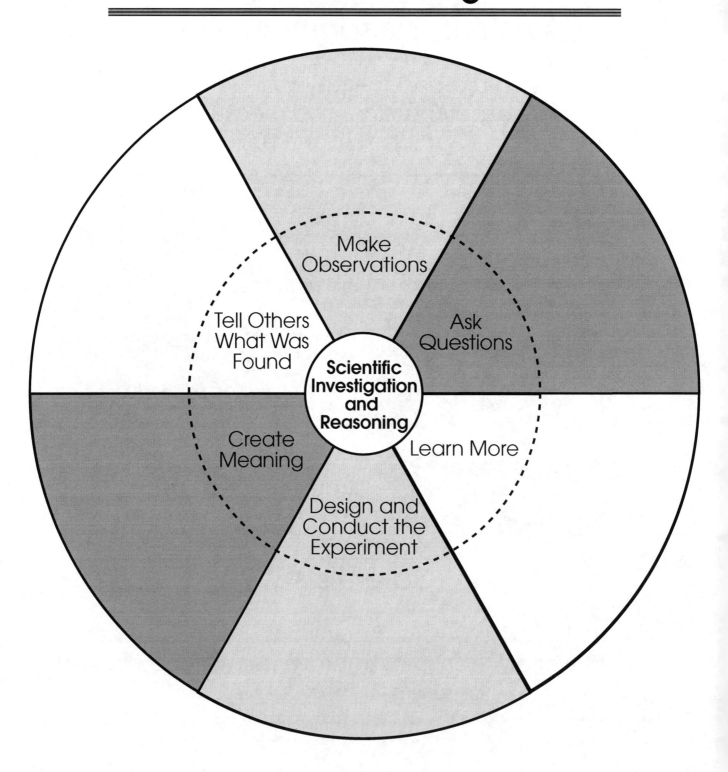

# Lesson 2:
# What Is Change?

## Planning the Lesson

### Instructional Purpose
- To understand the concept of change.
- To learn four generalizations about change that will deepen understanding of the sun, shadows, and conservation.

### Instructional Time
- 45 minutes

### Change Concept Generalizations
- Change is everywhere.
- Change is related to time.
- Change can be natural or manmade.
- Change may be random or predictable.

### Scientific Investigation Skills and Processes
- Make observations.

### Assessment "Look Fors"
- Students can give examples of things that change.
- Students can give examples of things that don't change.
- Students can apply change generalizations.
- Students can use size, comparison, and time/sequence concepts to describe change.

### Materials/Resources/Equipment
- Lab coat for teacher
- One lab coat (white adult T-shirt or dress shirt) for each student
- Enlarged picture of the teacher as a baby or young child
- Charts created using Handouts 2A (Things That Change) and 2B (Change Rules or Generalizations)
- Two large sticky notes for each pair of students
- Pencils
- Chart paper with the heading Things That Don't Change
- Copy of Handout 2C (Change Is Everywhere) for each student

> **Note to Teacher:**
> Some nonexamples of change include time, gravity, and the past. It may be helpful to post a chart with the change generalizations in the classroom.

## Implementing the Lesson

1. Put on lab coats. Explain to students that they are going to learn to "think like a scientist" and learn how to use their senses to make observations.
2. Ask students to share their parents' responses to the prompt from the homework assigned during the previous lesson:
   - What would you investigate/do if you were a scientist?

3. Show students a picture of you as a baby or child without revealing that it is a picture of you. Lead the students to discover the identity of the person in the picture by asking the following questions:
   - Who do you think this person is?
   - What clues could you use to help you identify this person?
   - Who in this room looks like this person? In what ways?

4. Reveal that the child in the picture is you as a child and lead the students to discuss how you have changed using the following questions:
   - In what ways have I changed since I was the child in this picture?
   - In what ways have I not changed?
   - How can you tell that the child in the picture is me?
   - Turn to a partner and describe how you have changed from when you were a baby to now.

5. Tell students that they just observed how you have changed since you were a child and that scientists also make observations about change. In fact, scientists spend a lot of time either trying to explain why a change occurred or causing a change to occur. Studying change is one of the most important things scientists do. Ask students:
   - Why do you think that it is important for scientists to study change?
   - How do you think scientists study change?

6. Display the chart of Handout 2A. Tell the students that people are not the only things that change in our world—many other things change as well. Point to the categories of change on the chart: (1) changes in people, (2) changes in animals, (3) changes on land, (4) changes in the sky, (5) changes in the water, (6) changes where people live and work, and (7) other changes. Provide one example of a change (according to 1 of the 7 categories on the chart). Write/draw that change on a large sticky note. Ask students to tell you what kind of change you described. Place the sticky note in the appropriate column on the chart.

7. Pair the students and give each student a large sticky note. Ask each pair to either draw or write about a change and to think about what kind of change it is. Explain that the students are to come up with a different example than the one you gave. Circulate as the pairs work and provide guidance when necessary.

8. Discuss what it means to classify things. Scientists sort and classify to help them understand something they are investigating. Model how you classified your example of change and tell the students that you want them to do the same.

9. Ask each student pair to share their example of change and classify it by placing the sticky note in the appropriate column on the chart. Guide students in their classifications and praise unusual examples of change. Add columns to the chart for other categories of change that students might identify.

10. Display a piece of chart paper with the heading Things That Don't Change. Have students turn to a partner and identify something that does not change. Ask pairs to share their example and write pairs' responses on the chart Things That Don't Change. Discuss whether it was easier to think of examples of things that change or things that do not change.

11. Explain that scientists use what they know about change when they are investigating. After looking at different examples of change, there are certain things that we know are true about all changes—these are "rules" for change

or generalizations about change. For example, one rule or generalization might be "change is everywhere."

12. Present the following generalizations by posting the chart of Handout 2B. Explain that students will be looking at how these generalizations or rules help scientists understand changes in the sun, shadows, and our world:
    - Change is everywhere.
    - Change is related to time.
    - Change can be natural or manmade.
    - Change may be random or predictable.

13. Model how the change generalizations apply to the changes that have occurred since you were the child in the picture. Ask students also to share how the generalizations apply to how you have changed with this question:
    - Look at the rules or generalizations about change; how do they explain the changes in me since I was the child in this picture?

14. Pass out the student log books. Ask students to date a second entry and respond to one of two prompts:
    - One natural change in me is . . .

OR

    - An example of a change I have caused is . . .

## Concluding and Extending the Lesson

### Concluding Questions and/or Actions
- How do scientists help us by studying change?
- Do you think change is a good thing or a bad thing? Describe why you feel that way.
- If you were a scientist, what changes would you like to study?

### What to Do at Home
- Ask the students to complete the Change Is Everywhere handout (Handout 2C) and bring it to the next science class.

Name: _____     Date: _____

# Things That Change

## Things That Change

| Changes in People | Changes in Animals | Changes on Land | Changes in the Sky | Changes in the Water | Changes Where We Live and Work | Other Changes |
|---|---|---|---|---|---|---|
| | | | | | | |

**Handout 2B**

# Change Rules or Generalizations

- Change is everywhere.

- Change is related to time.

- Change can be natural or manmade.

- Change may be random or predictable.

Name: _____

Date: _____

# Change Is Everywhere

Draw and label four things that change in your house.

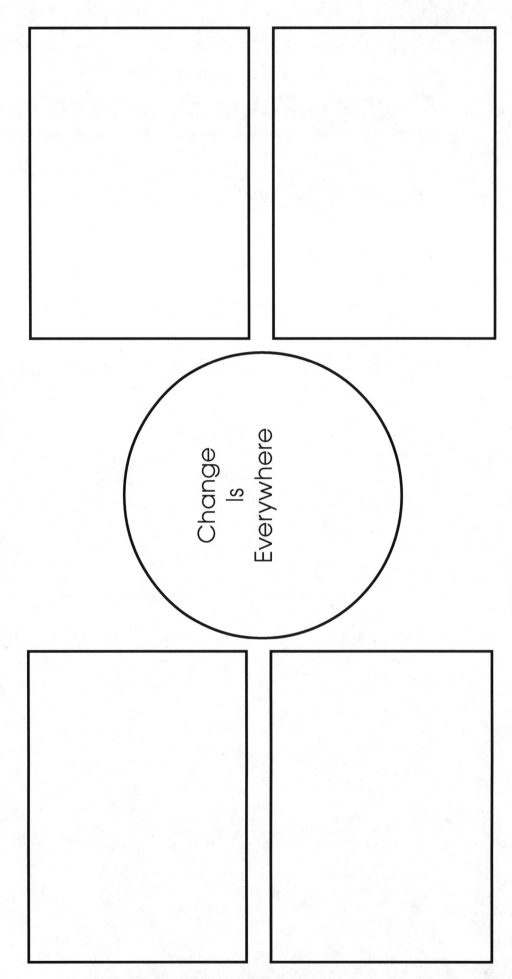

Change
Is
Everywhere

# Lesson 3:
# What Scientists Do—Observe, Question, Learn More

## Planning the Lesson

### Instructional Purpose
- To learn about the Wheel of Scientific Investigation and Reasoning.
- To apply three of six investigation processes (make observations, ask questions, and learn more) to investigate how shadows are produced.

### Instructional Time
- 45 minutes

### Change Concept Generalizations
- Change can be natural or manmade.

### Key Science Concepts
- Shadows can occur whenever light is present.
- Shadows can be produced when light is blocked.

### Scientific Investigation Skills and Processes
- Make observations.
- Ask questions.
- Learn more.
- Design and conduct the experiment.
- Create meaning.
- Tell others what was found.

### Assessment "Look Fors"
- Students can use size, comparison, and time/sequence concepts to describe observations.
- Students can apply the scientific investigation processes.
- Students understand how shadows are produced.

### Materials/Resources/Equipment
- Lab coat for teacher
- One lab coat (white adult T-shirt or dress shirt) for each student
- Chart or slide of Handout 1B from Lesson 1
- Chart paper, slide, or sentence strip with the question "Why did the shadow change?"
- Flashlight or lamp
- Tennis ball
- Chart paper
- Student log books

## Implementing the Lesson

1. Put on lab coats. Explain to students that they are going to learn to "think like a scientist" using the processes of scientific investigation.
2. Ask students to share their responses from the homework assigned during the previous lesson (Handout 2C).
3. Ask students what they think it means when we say that scientists "investigate" something. Explain that to investigate something means you find out as much as you can about it. Ask students:
   - Have you ever investigated something?
   - What did you investigate?
   - How did you investigate?

4. Use the wheel (Handout 1B) to review the six processes introduced in Lesson 1 and explain that scientists do these things to "investigate": (1) make observations, (2) ask questions, (3) learn more, (4) design and conduct experiments, (5) create meaning, and (6) tell others what was found. Remind students that scientists use these processes when learning about their world.
5. Show students a flashlight (or other light source) and an opaque object, such as a tennis ball. Tell students that they are going to conduct a shadow investigation using the flashlight and tennis ball.
6. Point to the Make Observations section on the wheel. Tell students that the first thing scientists do is use their senses to learn about something. Turn out the lights so that the room is completely dark or as dark as possible. Place the flashlight or other light source directly on the stool or table and turn it on. Have students observe the ball's shadow when it is 1 foot from the light source. Pause. Move 2 more feet from the ball. Pause. Again, move 2 feet away from the ball (i.e., the ball is now 5 feet from the light source). Ask students:
   - When you make observations, you use your senses to learn. What sense do you use the most to make observations?
   - What observations did you make?
   - How did the shadow change?

7. Point to the Ask Questions section on the wheel. Help students understand the difference between making a statement and asking a question. Model sample questions and statements based on Lesson 1. Then model your question for this lesson, recording it on the board, slide, sentence strip, or chart paper:
   - Why did the shadow change?

8. Have students think about questions they could ask about the shadow on the wall. If students make a statement, rephrase the statement as a question. Write the students' questions on chart paper.
9. Point to the Learn More section of the wheel. Ask students how they can gather information to learn more about a topic. Encourage them to think of the many ways people learn. Emphasize that the more they observe something the more they can learn about it. Ask students what they noticed about the size of the shadow as the object moved farther from the light. Repeat the earlier demonstration. Engage students in a discussion using the following questions as a guide:
   - When you want to learn more about something what do you do?
   - How are shadows formed?

- What did you notice about the size of the shadow as the ball moved farther from the light?
- What other questions do you have about shadows that are not already on our list?

10. Tell students that they are going to learn more about shadows through investigation. Distribute the student log books and ask the students to date and make another entry (drawn or written) using the following prompt:
- I noticed that the shadows . . .

## Concluding and Extending the Lesson

### Concluding Questions and/or Actions
- Share log entries about what students noticed.
- What do you think caused the shadow to change?

### What to Do at Home
- Ask students to observe and identify shadows in their home and to think about the questions: "Where were the shadows?" and "How were the shadows alike and how were they different?"

# Lesson 4:
# What Is a Shadow?

## Planning the Lesson

### Instructional Purpose
- To investigate how shadows occur.
- To analyze how shadows change as the direction of the light source changes.

### Instructional Time
- 45 minutes

### Change Concept Generalizations
- Change is related to time.
- Change can be natural or manmade.

### Key Science Concepts
- Shadows can occur whenever light is present.
- Shadows can be produced when light is blocked.
- Changes in the sun and shadows can be observed and measured.

### Scientific Investigation Skills and Processes
- Make observations.
- Learn more.

### Assessment "Look Fors"
- Students can describe and explain how shadows are produced.
- Students can describe and analyze how shadows can change due to the direction of the light source.
- Students can use comparison and direction/position concepts to describe shadows.

### Materials/Resources/Equipment
- Lab coat for teacher
- One lab coat (white adult T-shirt or dress shirt) for each student
- Chart or slides of Handouts 1B, 4A (Learning More About Shadows), 4B (Definition of Shadow), and 4C (My Observation of Shadows)
- Copies of Handout 4C, one for each student, or two pieces of plain paper for younger students
- Flashlight
- Stick of modeling clay or can of playdough
- New pencil
- Dark room
- *Light: What Is a Shadow?* by Jim Pipe (optional)
- *What Is a Shadow? Projects About Light* by Jackie Holderness (optional)

## Implementing the Lesson

1. Put on lab coats and ask students to share their findings generated from the previous day's assignment. Ask students:
   - What shadows did you observe at home?
   - What did you notice about the shadows?
   - Where were the shadows?
   - How were the shadows alike and different?

2. Review Lesson 3 on three scientific investigation processes—(1) make observations, (2) ask questions, and (3) learn more—by asking students:
   - What do scientists do before they do an experiment?
   - What question did we have about shadows? ("Why did the shadow change?")
   - What did you learn about shadows from the previous lesson?

3. Call students attention to the Learn More section of the wheel (Handout 1B). Indicate that students are going to apply the Learn More section of the wheel to the day's lesson. Remind students that before doing an experiment it is important for scientists to learn more about the question that they have. Post a piece of chart paper with the chart on it (Handout 4A). Explain the chart and quickly engage the class in identifying what they already know about shadows, what they want to know about shadows, and how they could learn about shadows. Write student responses in the corresponding column.

4. Explain that scientists often learn more about something by making more observations. Refer the students back to their chart with the questions they had about shadows. Ask students:
   - What more do you want to learn about shadows?

5. Begin by placing the lump of clay or playdough on a small table and rolling it into a ball. Place a pencil into the lump so that it is sticking straight up and down.

6. Gather students in a centralized location in the classroom near a wall. Tell students to observe the demonstration carefully.

7. Turn off all the lights and make the room as dark as possible. Hold the flashlight directly over the top of the pencil so that it is shining straight down. State your actions to the students, focusing on direction/position concepts, such as "I am holding the flashlight *above* the pencil." Pause and have students briefly remark upon their observations, using the following prompts:
   - What occurs when light is shone onto an object from above?
   - What do you think will happen if I move the light source?

8. Slowly move the flashlight toward the tabletop, keeping it about 1 foot from the pencil. Ensure that the light points toward the pencil at all times. State the direction of your movement and final position as you move the light. Pause once again and have students remark upon their observations. Ask students:
   - What occurs as light moves from above an object to the side of the object?

9. Turn on the lights. Ask students to relate the demonstration with their own observations and experiences with shadows, using the following questions:
   - Where have you seen shadows?
   - What caused the shadows to appear?

- Were the shadows long or short?
- Why do you think shadows can change size?

10. Engage students in a discussion to provide them an opportunity to explain and define the concept of shadows. Use Handout 4B to define shadow as "a darkened area made by something blocking out light" (Scholastic, 2007).

## Concluding and Extending the Lesson

### Concluding Questions and/or Actions

- How are shadows created?
- Why do shadows change?
- What new questions do you have about shadows?
- Go outside and ask students to go on a hunt for shadows (Handout 4C). Each student should identify the shadows of two stationary items and record the date, time, and a description of the shadow in their science investigation log. Allow students to observe and describe the shadows of the same two items at two different times and record their observations in their log books.
- Ask students to draw a picture showing how they can create either a long shadow or a short shadow, showing the direction of the light source.
- Set up a shadow investigation center with a flashlight and various objects. Allow students to investigate how shadows change as the direction of the light source changes.

> **Note to Teacher:** Instead of using Handout 4C, you can use blank sheets of paper for each observation and have students draw and label what the sun looks like and what the shadow looks like for each shadow object.

### What to Do at Home

- Send home a family newsletter requesting that an adult take the child on a moonlight walk. Ask the students to think about their shadow at night and to describe the size and shape of their shadow at night. Allow students to share their observations with classmates.

Name: _____

Date: _____

# Learning More About Shadows

| What we KNOW about shadows | What we WANT to know about shadows | How we can LEARN about shadows |
|---|---|---|
|  |  |  |

Name:_____ Date:_____

# Definition of Shadow

A shadow is . . .

"a dark shape made by something blocking out light."

Handout 4C

# My Observations of Shadows

| | Shadow Object #1 | Shadow Object #2 |
|---|---|---|
| Date: | The sun is . . . | The sun is . . . |
| Time: | The shadow looks . . . | The shadow looks . . . |
| Date: | The sun is . . . | The sun is . . . |
| Time: | The shadow looks . . . | The shadow looks . . . |

# Lesson 5:
# What Scientists Do—Experiment, Create Meaning, Tell Others

## Planning the Lesson

### Instructional Purpose
- To apply the Wheel of Scientific Investigation and Reasoning to design and conduct an experiment about how shadows are produced, to create meaning from the experiment, and to tell others what was found.

### Instructional Time
- 45 minutes

### Change Concept Generalizations
- Change is everywhere.
- Change is related to time.
- Change can be natural or manmade.
- Change may be random or predictable.

### Key Science Concepts
- Shadows can be produced when light is blocked.
- Shadows can occur whenever light is present.
- Changes in the sun and shadows can be observed and measured.

### Scientific Investigation Skills and Processes
- Design and conduct the experiment.
- Create meaning.
- Tell others what was found.

### Assessment "Look Fors"
- Students can use size, comparison, and time/sequence concepts to describe observations.
- Students can apply the steps of scientific investigation.
- Students can interpret data from a data table.
- Students can describe how the experiment was conducted and what results were found.
- Students understand how shadows are produced.

### Materials/Resources/Equipment
- Lab coat for teacher
- One lab coat (white adult T-shirt or dress shirt) for each student
- Charts or slides of Handouts 1B, 5A (Definition of Hypothesis), 5B (Using a Question to Form a Hypothesis), 5C (Steps for Shadow Experiment), and 5D (Shadow Experiment Data)
- Copies of Handout 5E (Science Investigation Badges)
- Student work using Handout 4C
- Chart paper

- Flashlight or lamp without a shade
- Yardstick
- Masking tape
- Tennis ball
- Pencil or marker
- Student log books

## Implementing the Lesson

1. Ask the students to think about what they learned about shadows during their moonlight walk. Allow students to share their observations with another classmate. In pairs, ask them to describe the size and shape of their shadow at night. Review responses from a couple of pairs of students, then ask the pairs to infer why there might not have been a shadow at night.

2. Put on lab coats and review what the class did during the previous lessons (Lessons 3 and 4), making sure to review student findings using Handout 4C. Ask students:
   - What did we start to investigate during the past two science classes?
   - What did we do to begin our investigation of shadows?
   - What did we observe about shadows over time?

3. Call students' attention to Design and Conduct the Experiment on the wheel (Handout 1B). Note that the first thing scientists do to conduct an experiment is to form a hypothesis from their question. Use Handout 5A to define hypothesis as "a temporary prediction that can be tested about how a scientific investigation or experiment will turn out" (Scholastic, 2007). Use Handout 5B to model your thinking process in turning your original question into a hypothesis.

4. Have students either turn to their partner or talk in small groups about other possible hypotheses that could come from the question and write down the hypotheses on chart paper.

5. Explain that the hypothesis needs to be tested. Ask students what they think "test the hypothesis" means. Encourage students to share how they think the class could find out whether the prediction or hypothesis is true by measuring the shadow's size as the object moves farther from the light.

6. Explain that it is important to plan the experiment by listing the steps. Ask students what steps they would take. After students share, reveal the list of steps the class is going to follow (see Handout 5C). Point out the list of materials that are needed for the experiment.

7. Explain that scientists conduct an experiment more than once to make sure that what occurred is not just a coincidence. An experiment will only work if almost everything is the same in all of the trials. This means only one change can take place per trial. Show students how you set up a measuring tape to ensure that the object is an exact distance from the light each time you record its size. Explain that the class will conduct the experiment three times.

8. Conduct the experiment three different times, inviting students to assist with the experiment. Record the measurements using a chart or slide of Handout 5D. Ask students:
   - What do you notice about the measurements of the different shadows?
   - Were the measurements the same at the three different distances?
   - Why do you think the measurements are different?

9. Tell students that they have just conducted a scientific investigation or experiment. They tested their hypothesis and now they need to do the last two processes: (1) create meaning, and (2) tell others what was found. Point to these two sections of the wheel (Handout 1B).

10. Explain that to create meaning students should look at the shadow measurements or data that are written on Handout 5D. Scientists use charts or tables to look at data and analyze or figure out what it means. Ask students:
    - What did you observe about the size of the shadows as the ball was moved farther from the light?
    - What might have caused the difference?
    - Was our hypothesis or prediction correct?
    - What other questions do you have?
    - What other experiments do you think we might do?

11. Explain that the class needs to tell others what was found. Ask students what they think should be told about the shadow experiment and model what you would say. Then provide time for student pairs to choose one person they want to tell about the shadow experiment. Also allow the pairs to "practice" what they will say. Facilitate as needed. Ask students:
    - What do you think we should tell others about our shadow experiment?
    - Why do you think it is important to share this?

12. Proclaim that the students are scientists because they just conducted a scientific investigation. Pass out badges saying "I Conducted an Experiment in Science—Ask Me About It" (Handout 5E). Also ask students to date and make the following entry in their student log books:
    - When we did the shadow experiment I observed . . .

## Concluding and Extending the Lesson

### Concluding Questions and/or Actions
- If you did this experiment again, what would you do differently?
- What do you think our experiment showed us about change?
- Share student log book entries.
- Set up a shadow experiment station with a flashlight, different objects, a yardstick, a ruler, paper, and pencils. Allow students the opportunity to practice making shadows. Ask them to look at how the shadows change when the object is various distances from the light.
- Ask students to create their own pictures of key concepts from this lesson. Have them connect two of the pictures and tell why and how they are connected.

### What to Do at Home
- Test the class hypothesis at home by repeating the experiment for someone. Be prepared to tell if you found the same thing that the class found.

# Definition of Hypothesis

# A hypothesis is . . .

"a temporary prediction that can be tested about how a scientific investigation or experiment will turn out."

(Scholastic, 2007)

# Using a Question to Form a Hypothesis

## My Question . . .

What caused the shadow to get larger or smaller?

## I Learned More . . .

I learned that a shadow is a dark shape made by something blocking out light.

I observed that the shadow of an object may change.

## I Now Think . . .

A shadow changes when the object making the shadow is moved closer or farther away from light.

## My Prediction or Hypothesis . . .

When an object is closer to the light it creates a larger shadow than when it is farther from the light.

# Steps for Shadow Experiment

**Hypothesis:** When an object is closer to the light it creates a larger shadow than when it is farther from the light.

## Experiment Steps:
1. Find a lamp without a shade or a flashlight.
2. Find a tennis ball.
3. Use a yardstick to measure 1 foot from the light and place a mark on the floor.
4. Use a yardstick to measure 2 feet from the light and place a mark on the floor.
5. Use a yardstick to measure 3 feet from the light and place a mark on the floor.
6. Have one partner hold the ball in front of the light at the 1-foot mark.
7. The other partner should measure the shadow and write down the measurements.
8. Hold the ball in front of the light at the 2-foot mark.
9. Measure the shadow and write down the measurements.
10. Hold the ball in front of the light at the 3-foot mark.
11. Measure the shadow and write down the measurements.
12. Repeat the experiment three times using the same ball, the same light, and the same markings on the floor.

## Materials Needed:
- Lamp or flashlight
- Tennis ball
- Yardstick
- Masking tape
- Chart to write down measurements
- Pencil or marker

Name:_____ Date:_____

# Shadow Experiment Data

| | Shadow with ball at 1 foot | Shadow with ball at 2 feet | Shadow with ball at 3 feet |
|---|---|---|---|
| Trial 1 | | | |
| Trial 2 | | | |
| Trial 3 | | | |

## Conclusions:

We observed that . . .

_____

_____

_____

_____

# Science Investigation Badges

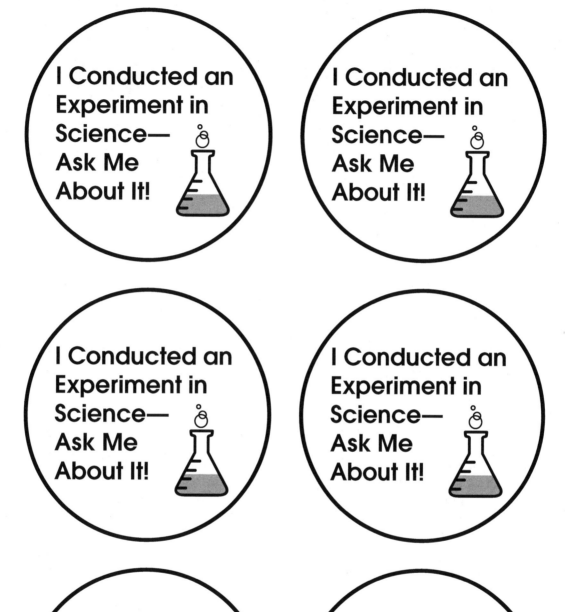

# Lesson 6:
# Shed a Little Light on Me

## Planning the Lesson

### Instructional Purpose
- To distinguish between natural and manmade sources of light.
- To understand how scientific investigation leads to discoveries or inventions that improve our world, such as the light bulb, a manmade light source invented by Thomas Edison.

### Instructional Time
- 45 minutes

### Change Concept Generalizations
- Change can be natural or manmade.
- Change may be random or predictable.

### Key Science Concepts
- Shadows can occur whenever light is present.
- Shadows can be produced when light is blocked.
- The sun is a natural source of heat and light.
- Natural resources help humans.

### Scientific Investigation Skills and Processes
- Ask questions.

### Assessment "Look Fors"
- Students can sequence the progression from natural to manmade light sources.
- Students can identify and explain sources of light that produce shadows.
- Students can explain how change was created with the invention of the light bulb.
- Students can describe how scientific investigation helps to improve the quality of our lives.

### Materials/Resources/Equipment
- Lab coat for teacher
- One lab coat (white adult T-shirt or dress shirt) for each student
- Charts or slides of Handouts 1B and 6A (Light Sources Chart)
- Slide or copies of Handout 6B (Shadows Concept Map; one for each student)
- *Young Thomas Edison* by Michael Dooling
- Student log books

## Implementing the Lesson

1. Put on lab coats and review what has been learned about shadows during the previous lessons. Ask students:

- How are shadows created?
- What causes shadows to change?
- What light caused the shadow on the wall in our classroom?
- What light caused the shadows that were observed outside?
- What is the difference between the shadows that we observed outside and the shadows that we produced on the wall of our classroom? (Look for answers such as the sun caused the shadows outside and a light caused the shadow inside.)

2. Remind students that *light* is needed to make a shadow. Ask students to identify both natural and manmade *light sources* and write student responses on the chart of Handout 6A. Make sure that the sun and moon are identified as natural light sources, and streetlights, lamps, or other relevant examples are provided as manmade light sources.

3. Turn off the classroom lights and darken the room as much as possible. Explain that thousands of years ago people lived on Earth and the only light they had was the natural light that came from the sun, moon, and stars. Ask students to imagine what it must have been like to live back then, using these questions:
- If the sun, moon, and stars were the only sources of light for you, how would you live your life differently than you do today?
- How would you feel at nighttime? What could you do at nighttime?
- Would you see shadows in the daytime? Why or why not?
- Would you see shadows in the nighttime? Why or why not?
- Describe whether you think life would be better if all we had were sun, moon, and star light.

4. Read the book, *Young Thomas Edison*, by Michael Dooling. Explain how scientific investigations often result in inventions that improve our lives. Use the following prompts to create discussion:
- Explain what Thomas Edison did that made him a scientist.
- What did Thomas Edison investigate?
- How did Thomas Edison change our world?
- Which generalization of change applies?

5. Darken the room again and demonstrate the difference in light that comes from a candle and light from a light bulb. Ask students:
- What do you think life would be like if Thomas Edison did not invent the light bulb?

6. Encourage students to think about whether or not shadows are different when created by natural or manmade sources. Ask students to tell how they might find this out. Encourage students to observe shadows made by natural light and those by manmade light. Ask students:
- Do you think shadows would be different if they were created by manmade sources versus natural light sources?
- How do you think you can find out?

7. Remind students that scientists make observations and identify questions that are based upon their observations. Pass out student log books and divide students into pairs. Provide time for them to observe shadows made by natural sources and those made by manmade sources. Have them draw or write about what they see in their log books.

8. Tell the student pairs that they are to think of a question they have after making their observations. If necessary, explain the difference in a statement and question.

9. Turn to the Concept Mapping Section in Appendix B as a guide for instructing students in concept mapping. To begin this activity, tell students: "We have just finished studying about shadows. Now we will review what we have learned. I am going to teach you how to show what you have learned in a way that will help you remember." Show them the slide of Handout 6B or distribute copies of Handout 6B. Tell students: "We know that shadows can be natural or manmade." Use the following questions as a guide for completing the concept map activity and use the completed concept map in Figure 2 as a guide.

   • What can we say about shadows?
   • What did we learn about the types of light needed to create shadows?

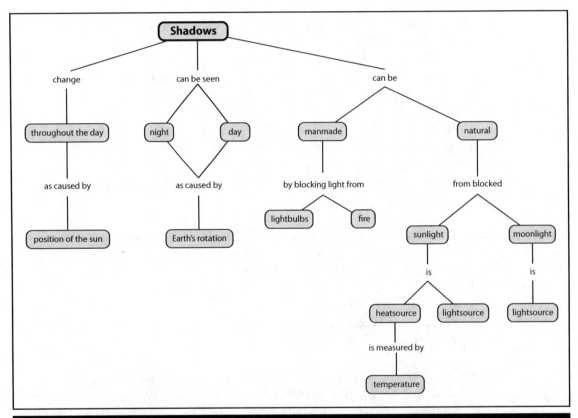

**Figure 2.** Completed concept map.

## Concluding and Extending the Lesson

### Concluding Questions and/or Actions

   • What did you learn about shadows that you did not know before today?
   • How have light sources changed? Do you think the change has been orderly or random? (After observations, ask each pair of students to write down on a sentence strip one question they have about shadows made from manmade and natural sources. Have student pairs share the question and reframe questions if necessary.)
   • Ask students to create timelines of the progression from natural to artificial light.

## What to Do at Home

- Ask the students to identify varied light sources in and around their home and identify whether the sources are natural or manmade. Encourage the students to examine the shadows created by the varied light sources.

Name: _____  Date: _____

# Light Sources Chart

| Natural Light Sources | Manmade Light Sources |
| --- | --- |
| | |

Name:_____ Date:_____

# Shadows Concept Map

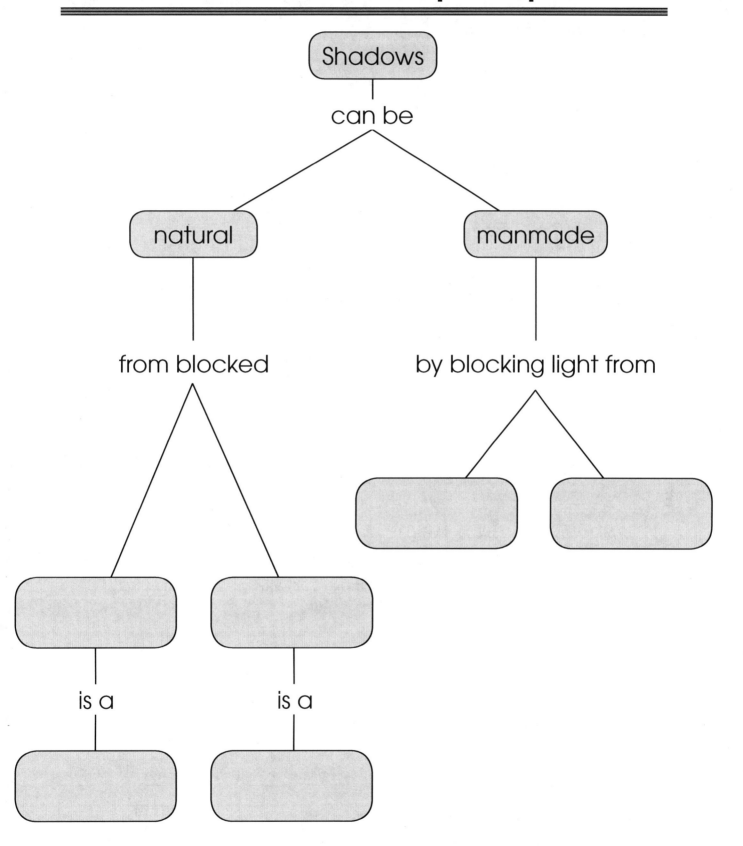

# Lesson 7:
# The Difference in Day and Night

## Planning the Lesson

### Instructional Purpose
- To understand that the Earth's rotation causes the appearance of day and night.
- To apply the change concept to examine how time is related to the movement of the Earth.

### Instructional Time
- 45 minutes

### Change Concept Generalizations
- Change is related to time.

### Key Science Concepts
- Changes in the sun and shadows can be observed and measured.
- Day and night are caused by the rotation of the Earth.

### Scientific Investigation Skills and Processes
- Learn more.

### Assessment "Look Fors"
- Students can demonstrate the Earth's counterclockwise rotation on its axis.
- Students understand that day and night are caused by the Earth's rotation on its axis.
- Students can analyze how time is related to the movement of the Earth and day and night.

### Materials/Resources/Equipment
- Lab coat for teacher
- One lab coat (white adult T-shirt or dress shirt) for each student
- Charts or slides of Handouts 7A (Comparing Day and Night), 7B (Definition of Rotation), and 7C (Sunrise and Sunset Chart)
- Toy car
- One ball/globe for each pair of students
- One flashlight for each pair of students
- One piece of drawing paper for each student
- Stickers
- Markers and/or crayons
- Bulletin board with the title "Look at Us During Sunrise, Noon, Dusk, and Midnight," with four labels for each time of day
- *Day and Night* by Anita Ganeri
- Student log books
- Internet access (optional)

## Implementing the Lesson

1. Put on lab coats and ask students to recall natural and manmade sources of light. Ask students to describe the difference in day and night using a Venn diagram (Handout 7A). Then ask students to turn to their partners and tell why they think we have day and night. Ask pairs to share what was discussed using the following questions:
   - What is the difference between day and night?
   - How would you describe day? How would you describe night?
   - What are some natural sources of light at night?
   - Why do you think we have day and night?

2. Read *Day and Night* by Anita Ganeri. Use the pictures to illustrate the changes that occur in the sky and on Earth and what people do as the Earth rotates around the sun. Guide students in naming changes that occur from day to night from the examples given in the book and using your own examples.

3. Practice the concept of rotation. Show students the wheels on a toy car or other object that rotates. Locate the center of the wheel. Ask students what they notice about the center of the wheel. Explain that the center stays in the same place but the edges turn. Using Handout 7B, define *rotate* as "to turn around and around like a wheel" (Scholastic, 2007). Mark a space on the floor for each student to stand on and practice rotating. Have students rotate in place on top of their target using small shuffling steps. Explain that the Earth rotates just like their movement. Ask students (they may also fill this in on Handout 7B):
   - What other things rotate or have parts that rotate?

4. Model the rotation of the Earth using a large globe and a flashlight. Explain to students that the globe represents the Earth and the flashlight represents the sun. Ask students to explain how the Earth rotates based on what they heard in the book and the last activity. Have a student volunteer hold the flashlight as you model the Earth rotating counterclockwise. Explain that the Earth is not straight up and down but tilts to the side. Change the position of the globe so that it is at an angle approximating 23°. Emphasize that the Earth's rotation causes day and night and that it takes 24 hours, or one day, for the Earth to rotate in a complete circle. Ask students:
   - When the globe turns, what do you notice about the light?
   - How are day and night created?

5. Divide the class into pairs and give each pair a flashlight and a ball or globe. Dim or turn off the lights so that the difference between the light and dark side is more distinct. Instruct one partner to be the sun and to hold the flashlight. The other partner will be the Earth and will rotate the ball counterclockwise in front of the sun, at an angle. (The Earth rotates around the sun at an angle of 23.5 degrees, but an exact angle measurement here is not necessary—you may just want to demonstrate to students serving as Earth how to hold their ball or globe.) Students will simulate the rotation of the Earth with their partners. Ask students:
   - Which part of the globe represents day and which part represents night?
   - How do you know this?

6. Ask students to name different times of day and write down the times on a piece of chart paper. Narrow down the list to sunrise/dawn, noon, sunset/twilight/dusk, and midnight. Explain that before there were clocks, people told time by the position of the sun. Using the globe and a single flashlight, locate where it would be sunrise/dawn, noon, sunset/twilight/dusk, and midnight. Discuss how, at the same moment, it is different times at different points on the Earth. The line between light and dark is called the terminator. Locate the terminator on the globe. Ask students:
    - What are you usually doing at sunrise or dawn? Noon? Sunset or dusk? Midnight?
    - Describe whether everyone in the world has day and night at the same time.

7. If Internet access is available, show students pictures of the terminator on the Earth and the moon at the following site: http://sci.gallaudet.edu/daylight.html
8. On one side of the globe place a sticker to mark the terminator. Explain to students that this represents a city at sunrise. Place a different sticker on the opposite side of the globe to represent a city at sunset. Slowly rotate the ball until the first sticker is in the center of the light. Ask students what time of day it is in both cities. Repeat this activity by rotating the globe to represent different times of day. Ask students:
    - How is change related to time? What changes occur from day to night?
    - How would your life change if the Earth did not rotate?

9. Discuss with students what the sun looks like from our perspective on Earth at different times of the day. Where is the sun at sunrise? (On the horizon.) Where is the sun at noon? (Overhead.)
10. Review the Venn diagram prepared at the beginning of class and make adjustments based on what the students have learned.
11. Divide the class into four groups and pass out pieces of plain drawing paper. Ask one group of students to draw a picture of themselves doing something at sunrise, with the correct position of the sun; another group at noon, with the correct position of the sun; the third group at sunset, with the correct position of the sun; and the last group at midnight.

## Concluding and Extending the Lesson

### Concluding Questions and/or Actions
- Have students share their pictures. Categorize their pictures according to time of day/night. Create a bulletin board to display student work titled, "Look at Us During Sunrise, Noon, Dusk, and Midnight."
- Pass out student log books. Ask students to respond to the prompt, "My favorite time of day or night is . . . because . . . "
- Remind students that scientists often use tables to create meaning from an investigation. For example, newspapers and weather reporters announce the time of sunrise and sunset. Show students a chart created from Handout 7C and model how to record the sunrise and sunset times. Continue to collect this data for 5 days. As the days progress, students can analyze the sunrise and sunset data to determine the patterns of change. They also can make predictions about sunrise and sunset times.

- Provide students with further opportunities to explore the rotation of the Earth around the sun by reading additional books.

### *What to Do at Home*

- Ask the students to listen to the weather report or have someone read the newspaper for sunrise and sunset times for 5 days. Have students record the data on the chart created from Handout 7C.

Name: _____

Date: _____

# Comparing Day and Night

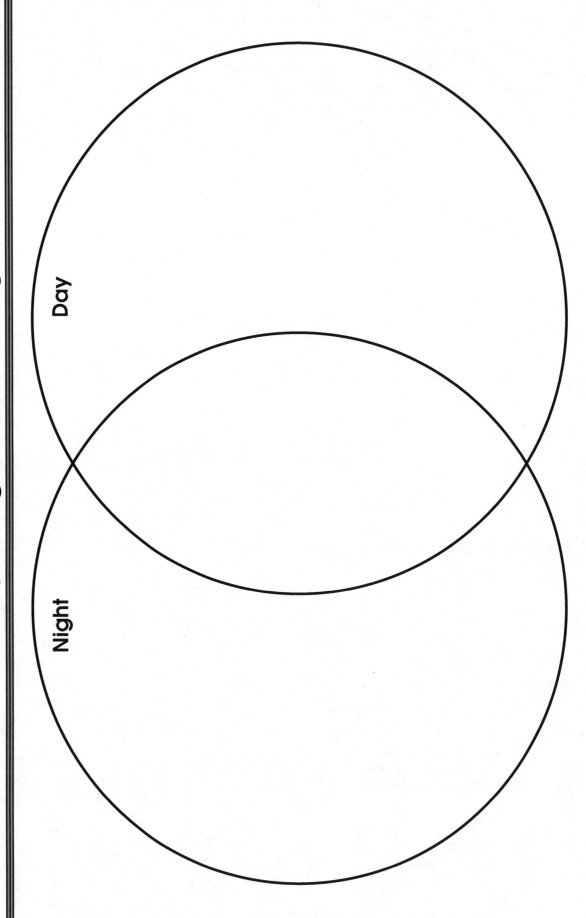

Day

Night

Name:_____ Date:_____

# Definition of Rotation

## Rotation . . .
### "to turn around and around like a wheel."
### (Scholastic, 2007)

Some things that rotate:

_____

_____

_____

_____

_____

_____

Name: _____ Date: _____

# Sunrise and Sunset Chart

| Day | Date | Sunrise Time | Sunset Time |
|-----|------|--------------|-------------|
|     |      |              |             |
|     |      |              |             |
|     |      |              |             |
|     |      |              |             |

Observations: _____

_____

# Lesson 8:
# Me and My Shadow

## Planning the Lesson

### Instructional Purpose
- To continue to explore the nature of shadows and the sun by making observations, asking questions, and learning more to investigate how long and short shadows are produced by the sun's position in the sky.

### Instructional Time
- 45 minutes

### Change Concept Generalizations
- Change is everywhere.
- Change can be natural or manmade.
- Change may be random or predictable.

### Key Science Concepts
- Shadows can occur whenever light is present.
- Shadows occur in nature when light is blocked by an object.
- Changes in the sun and shadows can be observed and measured.

### Scientific Investigation Skills and Processes
- Make observations.
- Ask questions.
- Learn more.

### Assessment "Look Fors"
- Students can describe and analyze how shadows can change based on the direction of the light source.
- Students can relate observed changes in shadows to generalizations about change.
- Students can use size, comparison, shape, and direction/position concepts to describe and analyze how shadows change.

### Materials/Resources/Equipment
- Lab coat for teacher
- One lab coat (white adult T-shirt or dress shirt) for each student
- Charts or slides of Handouts 1B, 8A (Shadow Predictions), and 8B (Shadow Investigation Question)
- Slide or copies of Handout 8C (Shadows Concept Map)
- Copies of Handout 8A, one per student
- *What Makes a Shadow?* by Clyde Robert Bulla
- Student log books
- Movie, *Peter Pan*

> **Note to Teacher:**
> Weather conditions will influence how you pursue this lesson. If it is cloudy, students will be able to make predictions but will not be able to see each other's shadows.

## Implementing the Lesson

1. Put on lab coats and call students' attention to the Make Observations, Ask Questions, and Learn More sections of the Wheel (Handout 1B). Also, note sunrise and sunset times on the chart introduced during the previous lesson (Handout 7C).

2. Briefly review with students what they have learned about light and shadows, using the following:
   - Describe how shadows are formed.
   - What different light sources create shadows?

3. Tell students: "We are going to create a new concept map about how shadows are seen." Show students a slide of Handout 8C or distribute copies of Handout 8C for student use. Point out the top of the concept map that shows that shadows can be seen. Use the completed concept map following the lesson in Figure 3 and the following questions to guide the students in completing the concept map:
   - What did we learn about shadows yesterday?
   - When can shadows be seen?
   - What causes the changes that come when shadows can be seen?

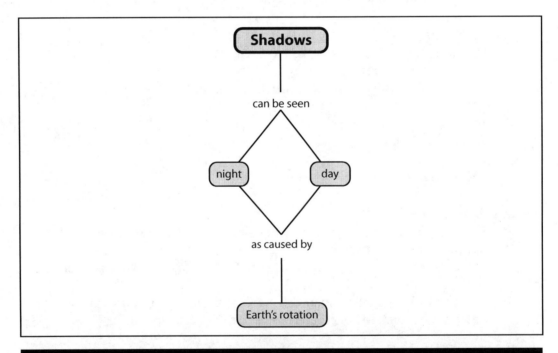

**Figure 3.** Completed concept map for shadows.

4. Ask students to recall when they have seen their own shadow. Use the following prompts to create a discussion:
   - What did your shadow look like?
   - What light sources created your shadow?
   - Describe whether you think your shadow changes and tell why and how it changes.
   - Why do they think shadows sometimes disappear?

5. Read aloud *What Makes a Shadow?* by Clyde Robert Bulla, pausing periodically to allow students to reflect upon the content. Reinforce direction/position and size concepts throughout the reading with the following questions:
   - When you are outside, how can you tell where the sun is by looking at the position of a shadow?
   - How can you make your shadow bigger? Smaller?

6. Pair up the students and explain that the pairs are going to go outside to observe and make comparisons of their shadows. Ask the pairs to predict whether they think they will see each other's shadows and whether they think that their shadows will look alike or look different. Ask the pairs to write their predictions on Handout 8A, which will become part of their student log books.

7. Allow pairs to go outside to observe each other's shadows and make comparisons. Then return indoors and process student findings using the following prompts:
   - Was your prediction correct? Were you able to observe each other's shadows? Why or why not?
   - Was your prediction about whether your shadows would be alike correct? How are your shadows alike? How are your shadows different?
   - Why do you think your shadows are alike? Why do you think your shadows are different?
   - Did a natural or a manmade light source produce the shadows?

8. Encourage discussion about whether the students' shadows would look the same if they went outside at another time of day. Pose the following question:
   - When my shadow is created by the sun, does it look the same at different times of the day? (See Handout 8B.)

## Concluding and Extending the Lesson

### Concluding Questions and/or Actions
- When can you predict that you will not be able to see your shadow outside?
- How could you change your shadow when you are outside?
- Is it possible for you to have the same shadow as your partner? Why or why not?
- Allow the students to go outside at a different time to observe their shadows.
- Ask students to complete the investigation log entry prompt included on Handout 8A: "Something I learned about shadows today is . . . "
- Provide a light source and a blank wall and give students the opportunity to experiment with changing their shadows and writing down how they changed their shadows in their log books.
- Show the clip from the movie Peter Pan where Peter is struggling with his shadow. Engage students in a discussion about why this would be impossible. Record student responses on a chart to help them in their studies of shadows.

### What to Do at Home
- Send home a family newsletter requesting that an adult take the child outdoors after school and then again in the evening. Ask the students to describe how the length of their shadow changed and why they think this occurred.

# Shadow Predictions

Date: _____

Names of Scientists: _____

_____

*Before* Going Outside, We Predict . . .

1. Our shadows_____ be seen.
      (will or will not)

2. Our shadows_____ look alike.
      (will or will not)

*After* Going Outside, We Found . . .

1. Our shadows_____ be seen.
      (could or could not)

2. Our shadows_____ look alike.
      (did or did not)

**What We Learned about Shadows Today:**

_____

_____

# Shadow Investigation Question

When my shadow is created by the sun, does it look the same at different times of the day?

Name:_____ Date:_____

# Shadows Concept Map

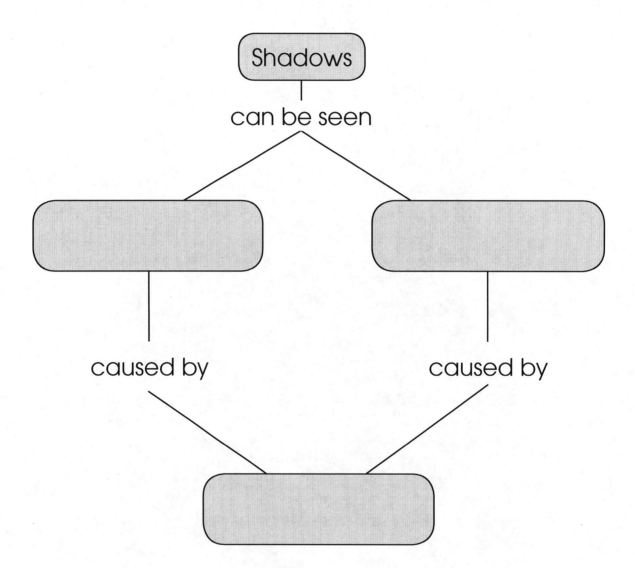

Shadows

can be seen

caused by

caused by

# Lesson 9:
# Watching Shadows Grow

## Planning the Lesson

### Instructional Purpose
- To design and conduct an experiment to investigate how the sun's direction at various times of the day affects the size and shape of shadows.

### Instructional Time
- Three 20-minute sessions (one in the morning, one at noon, and one in the afternoon) for a total of 60 minutes

### Change Concept Generalizations
- Change is related to time.

### Key Science Concepts
- Shadows can occur whenever light is present.
- Shadows occur in nature when light is blocked by an object.

### Scientific Investigation Skills and Processes
- Design and conduct the experiment.
- Create meaning.
- Tell others what was found.

### Assessment "Look Fors"
- Students can relate the direction and position of the sun to shadow length.
- Students can compare and contrast shadow lengths throughout the day.
- Students can describe how time creates changes in shadows.
- Students can use direction/position and time/sequence concepts to analyze and describe changes in shadows.
- Students can design and conduct an experiment.
- Students can interpret experiment findings and tell others.

### Materials/Resources/Equipment
- Lab coat for teacher
- One lab coat (white adult T-shirt or dress shirt) for each student
- Charts or slides of Handouts 1B, 5A, 5E, 8B, 9A (Steps for Morning, Noon, and Afternoon Shadow Experiment), and 9B (Watching Shadows Grow Data Table)
- Badges made from Handout 5E
- Markers
- White butcher paper
- One tape measure per pair of students
- One piece of colored chalk per pair of students
- Three sticky notes per pair of students

**Note to Teacher:**
This lesson requires you to take your children outside on three different occasions on a sunny day. It is best to take students outside early in the morning, around noon, and in the afternoon.

Ensure that students avoid looking directly at the sun. Discuss with students the harmful effects of doing so.

Prior to this lesson, students will need to know how to measure using a tape measure. If necessary, the lesson could be adapted by modeling the activity with three students.

## Implementing the Lesson

1. Put on lab coats and call students' attention to the Design and Conduct the Experiment, Create Meaning, and Tell Others What Was Found sections of the wheel (Handout 1B). Review the previous session and remind students of the question that was posed at the end of the lesson:
   - When my shadow is created by the sun, does it look the same at different times of the day?

2. Discuss with students their observations of their shadows from the home extension in the previous lesson using these questions:
   - What did your shadow look like in the daytime?
   - Did it change in the evening? If so, how did it change? Why do you think it changed?

3. Ask students how they could conduct an experiment on the question that has been posed.

4. Remind students that they need to make a hypothesis from the question and review the definition of hypothesis using Handout 5A and the following prompts:
   - What is a hypothesis?
   - What hypothesis can we make using our question, "When my shadow is created by the sun, does it look the same at different times of the day?"

5. Remind students that they need to write down the steps for the experiment. Ask students what they should do to conduct an experiment and help them to see that they can measure their shadows at several times during the day. Have students compare and contrast the steps they came up with to the steps on Handout 9A.

6. Pair up the students and display the Watching Shadows Grow Data Table (see Handout 9B). Inform students that the pairs will mark and then measure the length of their shadows three times during the day: in the morning, at noon, and in the afternoon. Designate one student to be the shadow maker and the other to be the shadow recorder. Have students measure and record the height of each shadow maker.

7. Ask students to predict the position of the sun in the morning. Then have students predict the relative length of their shadows based on the sun's position in the sky, relating this to previous investigations. Ask students:
   - Do you think your shadow will be shorter than or longer than your actual height in the morning? Why?

### Morning Measurement

8. Take students outside to an open, paved area (such as a basketball court). Have student pairs stand side-by-side, in a straight line, all facing their shadows. Mark a straight line in chalk at the toes of the students. Remind the students of their predictions. Model how the shadow maker stands on the line while the shadow recorder marks the "end" of the shadow maker's shadow using chalk and labeling the name of the shadow maker. Both students will use a tape measure to measure the length of the shadow from the line to the chalk mark and then write their measurement on a sticky note.

9. Tell students that they will return to the same location at noon to see if their shadows change.

10. Return to the classroom and post the shadow measurements on the chart created from Handout 9B, under the "Morning Shadow Measurement" heading.

### Noon Measurement

11. Review the purpose of the activity and students' observations of their shadows in the morning. Ask students:
    - Was your shadow shorter than, longer than, or about the same length as your actual height?
    - How do you know? (You might want to have students measure each others' heights at this point.)

12. Ask students to predict the position of the sun at midday and the relative length of their shadows based on the sun's position in the sky, relating this to previous investigations.

13. Return to the same location and have students face the line marking their morning shadows. Remind students of their predictions. Repeat the process used during the morning, having the shadow maker stand on the line and the shadow recorder mark the end of the shadow. Have each pair measure between the lines and write down their measurements on a sticky note.

14. Return to the classroom and post the shadow measurements on the chart created from Handout 9B, under the "Noon Shadow Measurement" heading.

### Afternoon Measurement

15. Return to the class chart at the end of the day. Ask students to comment on how the shadow changed from the morning to noon, using the following questions:
    - When was the shadow the shortest, in the morning or at noon?
    - Why do you think the shadow changed?

16. Ask students to predict the position of the sun in the afternoon. Have students predict the length of their shadows based on the sun's position in the sky.

17. Return to the same location as in the morning and at noon and have students face the lines marking their shadows. Remind students of their predictions. Repeat the process used previously, having the shadow maker stand on the line and the shadow recorder mark the end of the shadow. Have each pair measure between the lines and write down their measurements on a sticky note.

18. Return to the classroom and post the shadow measurements on the chart created from Handout 9B, under the "Afternoon Shadow Measurement" heading.

19. Have students compare and contrast the shadow measurements, asking the following:
    - When was the shadow shorter than the shadow maker's height?
    - When was the shadow longer? When was it closest to his or her actual height?

20. Point to the Create Meaning section on the wheel and ask students to infer why the shadow lengths changed throughout the day. Relate students' observations to the generalization about how change is related to time and the position of the sun. Engage students in a discussion about change using the following questions as a starting point:

- How do shadow lengths change throughout the day?
- Which generalizations about change apply to our experiment today?
- How will your shadow change as you grow older?

21. Point to the Tell Others What Was Found section on the wheel and have pairs practice what they will tell others about the day's experiment. Pass out badges created from Handout 5E.

## Concluding and Extending the Lesson

### Concluding Questions and/or Actions
- What question were we trying to answer today?
- What prediction or hypothesis was created?
- What did we do to test our hypothesis?
- Was our hypothesis correct?
- What conclusions or inferences could you draw from this investigation?
- Ask students to draw their shadow at a specific time of day. Students should note whether their shadow would be longer or shorter than they actually are.

### What to Do at Home
- Have students tell someone at home about the experiment that they conducted on shadows. Suggest to the students that they can repeat the experiment with someone at home.

Name:_____ Date:_____

## Handout 9A
# Steps for Morning, Noon, and Afternoon Shadow Experiment

**Hypothesis:** The sun creates different size shadows during the morning, noon, and afternoon.

### Experiment Steps:
1. Create a table for measurements.
2. Create pairs. Decide who will be the shadow maker and who will be the shadow recorder in each pair.
3. Go outside in the morning on a sunny day.
4. Have the shadow maker stand on the line.
5. Use a piece of chalk and have the shadow recorder mark the end of the shadow maker's shadow.
6. Use a tape measure to measure the length of the shadow maker's shadow.
7. Use the data table to record each pair's morning measurement.
8. Repeat steps 4–6 at noon.
9. Use the data table to record each pair's noon measurement.
10. Repeat steps 4–6 in the afternoon.
11. Use the data table to record each pair's afternoon measurement.
12. Compare and contrast the measurements during the morning, noon, and afternoon.

### Material Needed:
- Sun
- Blacktop or cement area
- Partners
- Chalk
- Tape measure
- Table for recording measurements

**91**

Name:_____ Date:_____

# Watching Shadows Grow Data Table

| Student Pairs | Morning Shadow Measurement | Noon Shadow Measurement | Afternoon Shadow Measurement |
|---|---|---|---|
| | | | |
| | | | |
| | | | |
| | | | |
| | | | |
| | | | |
| | | | |

# Lesson 10:
# Temperatures in Sun and Shade

## Planning the Lesson

### Instructional Purpose
- To design an experiment to investigate temperatures in sunny and shady locations to better understand the sun as a source of heat.

### Instructional Time
- 45 minutes

### Change Concept Generalizations
- Change can be natural or manmade.
- Change may be random or predictable.

### Key Science Concepts
- The sun is a natural source of heat and light.

### Scientific Investigation Skills and Processes
- Design and conduct the experiment.
- Create meaning.
- Tell others what was found.

### Assessment "Look Fors"
- Students can design and apply steps to conduct an experiment.
- Students can interpret data from a data table.
- Students can determine how shadows influence air temperature.

### Materials/Resources/Equipment
- Lab coat for teacher
- One lab coat (white adult T-shirt or dress shirt) for each student
- Charts or slides previously created of Handouts 1B, 4A, and 5A
- Charts or slides of Handouts 10A (Investigation Question for Temperature Experiment) and 10D (Sun and Shade Temperature Experiment Findings)
- Copies of Handouts 10B (Sun and Shade Temperature Experiment) and 10C (Sun and Shade Temperature Experiment Data Table), one per student
- Slide or copies of Handout 10F (Changing Shadows Concept Map)
- Badges made from Handout 5E
- Two thermometers for each group of 3–4 students
- Sunny day
- Shadow created by a large tree or building
- Student log books
- Copies of Handout 10E (Temperatures in the Sun and Shade Sample Graph; optional)

> **Note to Teacher:**
> Students will need to be taught how to read thermometers in order to complete this lesson successfully.
>
> You can differentiate this lesson by allowing more advanced learners to identify hypotheses and experiment steps independently, without Handouts 10B or 10C.

## Implementing the Lesson

1. Tell students: "We are going to create a new concept map about how shadows change." Show students a slide of Handout 10F or distribute copies of Handout 10F for student use. Point out the top of the concept map that shows that shadows change. Use the concept map in Figure 4 and the questions below to guide the students in completing the concept map:
   - When do shadows change?
   - What causes changes in shadows?

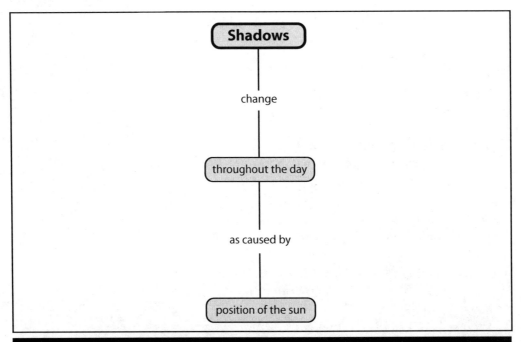

**Figure 4.** Completed concept map for how shadows change.

2. Put on lab coats and refer to the chart in Handout 4A to summarize what has been learned about shadows thus far. Note any questions that the class has not answered and find a way to link them to a question about whether the temperature is different in the sun and shade (Handout 10A). For example:
   - Something I still wonder about is, "Is the temperature in the shade hotter, cooler, or the same as the temperature in the sun?"

3. Use the Wheel of Scientific Investigation and Reasoning (Handout 1B) to recall what scientists do to investigate: (1) make observations, (2) ask questions, (3) learn more, (4) design and conduct the experiment, (5) create meaning, and (6) tell others what was found. Point to the Design and Conduct the Experiment section of the wheel.

4. Divide the class into small groups of 3 or 4 students and assign team numbers. Explain that you think they are ready to conduct an experiment more independently.

5. Point to the question "Is the temperature in the shade hotter, cooler, or the same as the temperature in the sun?" and remind student groups that they need to turn the question into a hypothesis using Handout 5A to review.

6. Pass out a copy of Handout 10B to each group. Encourage the students to link what they already know about the sun. Ask small groups to discuss whether or

not they believe the temperature is hotter, cooler, or the same in the shade as in direct sunlight and to complete the hypothesis prompt on Handout 10B.

7. Take a moment to explain that thermometers are instruments used to measure how hot or cold something is (temperature). Explain that the higher the number reads on the thermometer, the higher the air temperature is.

8. Ask small groups to discuss and decide what kind of experiment they could do to test their hypothesis using the thermometers. Discussion prompts include:
   - What is your hypothesis?
   - How could you use the thermometer to test your hypothesis?
   - Why do you think that might be a good experiment to do?

9. Ask each group to write down the experiment steps. Remind students that they will have to come up with a way to write down their data. Differentiate by allowing struggling students to use pictures or a tape recorder. Capable students may come up with their own table or chart, while struggling students could be given the Sun and Shade Temperature Experiment Data Table (Handout 10C) to record their findings. Ask students:
   - Think about what steps you need to take to do the experiment. What would you need to do first? Second? Next?
   - How are you going to record or write down the temperatures?

10. Take students outdoors to a location that has a large tree (or the shadow of a building) and an open area that is receiving direct sunlight. Allow the groups to conduct their experiments, making sure that they follow their experiment steps. Some groups may need extra assistance, and you can encourage these groups to put one thermometer in the shade and another in the sun. Monitor groups as they collect their data and assist with writing down their findings.

11. Return to the classroom and remind students that scientists collect information and data more than once to make sure that what they found was not just a coincidence. That is why several "teams" collected information about temperatures in sun and shade. The class can ask groups what they found and record their findings using Handout 10D. Ask students:
    - Was the temperature in the shade cooler, hotter, or the same as the temperature in the sun?
    - What was your hypothesis?
    - Was your hypothesis correct? If not, how could you change your hypothesis to make it correct?

12. Further the discussion by having students infer why air temperature is cooler in the shade. Afterwards, explain that shade is created by a shadow and is an area that is protected from the heat of sunlight. As an object blocks light, it also blocks heat, making it cooler than unprotected areas. Relate the word shade with shadow.

13. Tell students that they have just conducted a scientific investigation or experiment and ask the following questions to process the experience:
    - How do you think your experiment went?
    - How could you improve your experiment? (Steps complete? Right order? Necessary materials?)
    - How well did your team work together to do the experiment?
    - What was the hardest part of your experiment? What was the easiest?
    - How do you think changes to the environment such as chopping down trees affect temperature?

14. Proclaim that the student scientists have just conducted a scientific investigation and give out the badges from Handout 5E.

## Concluding and Extending the Lesson

### Concluding Questions and/or Actions
- What is something that you learned today about shadows that you did not know before?
- What did you learn about the temperature in the sun and shade?
- What change did the shadows produce?
- If you were outside and wanted to be cooler, what could you do?
- Pass out the investigation logs and ask students to respond to the prompt, "Today I learned/inferred/concluded . . . "
- Illustrate how scientists communicate data by using graphs. Provide direct instruction on how to create a bar graph of the temperature data collected in this investigation (see sample Handout 10E).

### What to Do at Home
- Send home a family newsletter suggesting that children conduct their own scientific investigation in which they measure and record temperature in different locations. Provide a time for students to share their home investigations.

# Investigation Question for Temperature Experiment

## Investigation Question:

Is the temperature in the shade hotter, cooler, or the same as the temperature in the sun?

# Sun and Shade Temperature Experiment

Team #_____ Scientists_____

_____

## Our Hypothesis:

The temperature in the shade will be

_____ as the temperature in the sun.

(hotter, cooler, the same)

## Experiment Steps:




## Materials We Will Need:

Name:_____ Date:_____

# Sun and Shade Temperature
# Experiment Data Table

**Team #_____ Scientists_____**

_____

| Temperature in the Sun | Temperature in the Shade |
|---|---|
|  |  |

Name:_____ Date:_____

# Sun and Shade Temperature Experiment Findings

| Team # | Temperature in the Sun | Temperature in the Shade |
|---|---|---|
|  |  |  |
|  |  |  |
|  |  |  |
|  |  |  |
|  |  |  |
|  |  |  |

Name:_____ Date:_____

# Temperatures in the Sun and Shade Sample Graph

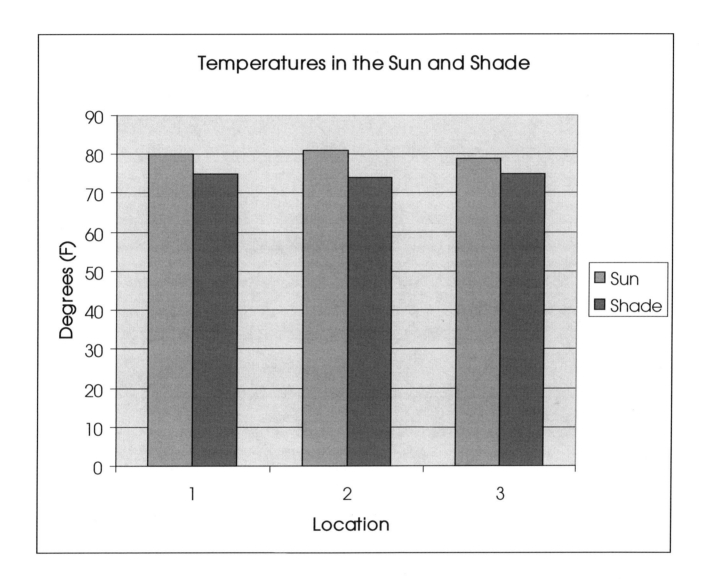

Name:_____ Date:_____

# Changing Shadows Concept Map

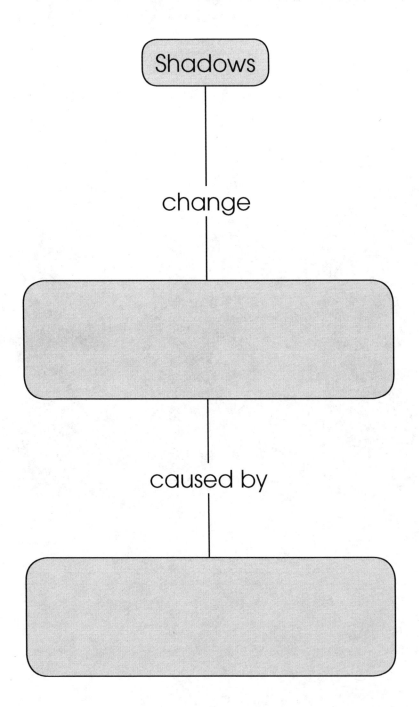

Shadows

change

caused by

# Lesson 11:
# The Greenhouse Effect

## Planning the Lesson

### Instructional Purpose
- To investigate the greenhouse effect that is produced by the sun and the Earth's atmosphere.
- To understand how the greenhouse effect helps to keep people warm.

### Instructional Time
- 45 minutes

### Change Concept Generalizations
- Change can be natural or manmade.

### Key Science Concepts
- The sun is a natural source of heat and light.
- Natural resources help humans.

### Scientific Investigation Skills and Processes
- Make observations.
- Design and conduct the experiment.
- Create meaning.
- Tell others what was found.

### Assessment "Look Fors"
- Students can describe how the greenhouse effect is produced by the sun.
- Students can determine how the greenhouse effect helps to keep us warm.
- Students can investigate and observe differences in temperatures in a simulation of the greenhouse effect.
- Students can use comparison, quantity, and time/sequence concepts to make observations.
- Students can identify the steps of scientific investigation.

### Materials/Resources/Equipment
- Lab coat for teacher
- One lab coat (white adult T-shirt or dress shirt) for each student
- Chart or slide previously created of Handout 1B
- Slide or copies of Handout 11A (Sunlight Concept Map; one per student)
- Slide of Handout 11B (Diagram of the Greenhouse Effect)
- Copies of Handout 11C (Temperature in a Jar Experiment Data Table; one for each group of 3–4 students)
- Two thermometers for each group of 3–4 students
- One glass jar for each group of 3–4 students
- Sunny area to perform the experiment
- Picture of a greenhouse (optional)
- *A True Book: The Ozone Layer* by Rhonda Lucas Donald (optional)
- Environmental Issues posters by McDonald Publishing (optional)

## Implementing the Lesson

1. Put on lab coats and review what was learned about temperature in the direct sunlight and in shadows. Point to the Make Observations, Design and Conduct the Experiment, Create Meaning, and Tell Others What Was Found sections of the wheel. Ask students:
   - What did we learn about the difference in the temperature in direct sunlight and in shadows?
   - Why is the temperature cooler in shadows than in the sun?

2. Tell students: "We are going to create a new concept map about sunlight." Show students a slide of Handout 11A or distribute copies of Handout 11A for student use. Point out the top of the concept map that shows sunlight. Use the concept map in Figure 5 and the questions below to guide the students in completing the concept map:
   - What kind of source is sunlight?
   - How is sunlight as a heat source measured?

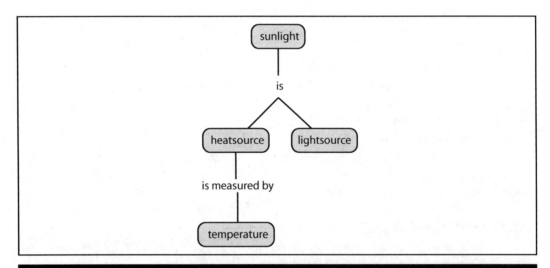

**Figure 5.** Completed concept map for sunlight.

3. Explain that there would be no life on Earth if we did not have the sun because the sun helps to keep us warm. Ask students to describe any experiences they have had with greenhouses. Explain that greenhouses look like small glass houses and that they are used to grow plants, especially in the winter. Greenhouses work by trapping heat from the sun. The glass in the greenhouse lets in light but keeps heat from escaping. If desired, you can show a picture of a greenhouse. Begin a discussion with students using the following questions as a guide:
   - Describe a time when you have been to a greenhouse. What was it like?
   - Was it warmer inside the greenhouse or outside the greenhouse?
   - Why do you think it was warmer inside the greenhouse?

4. Explain that the Earth has an atmosphere that helps keep the warmth created by the sun close to the Earth. The Earth's atmosphere keeps the heat that the sun produces from going into outer space. The class is going to observe how

the sun and the Earth's atmosphere work together to keep us warm on Earth. You can use a slide of the diagram presented on Handout 11B to explain.

5. Go outside to a sunny area and divide the class into groups of 3 or 4 students. Give each group two thermometers, one glass jar, and one copy of Handout 11C. Have the students wait for about 3 minutes so the thermometers will give accurate readings.

6. Explain that the Earth's atmosphere is like the glass jar and the students are going to observe how it holds in the sun's heat.

7. Instruct each group to put a glass jar over one of the thermometers and to leave the other thermometer out in the open. Explain that half of each small group will read the thermometer covered by the jar and the other half will read the thermometer that is not in the jar. Have teams decide who will do each task.

8. Explain that you are going to wait for 2 minutes and then, when you give the signal, each group will read its thermometer and write down the temperatures in the appropriate space on Handout 11C.

9. Repeat the process 3 or 4 times at 2-minute intervals so that the student groups have 3 or 4 readings.

10. Return inside and process what the students found, using these questions:
    - How did the temperature under the glass and the temperature outside the glass differ?
    - Why do you think the temperatures differed?
    - Describe whether you think the heating of the Earth is natural or manmade?

11. Explain that the air outside is constantly moving. As the air moves, warm air gets replaced by cooler air. But the air in the jar can't move like the air outside the jar. The air in the jar doesn't have enough fresh air to cool it so the air gets warmer and warmer. This is what happens in the Earth's atmosphere. The sun beats down on the Earth and warms the Earth's surface, and this heat gets trapped by the Earth's atmosphere.

12. Ask the students to discuss what they learned from the investigation.


## Concluding and Extending the Lesson

### Concluding Questions and/or Actions
- What did we investigate today?
- How did our experiment demonstrate what happens for the sun to heat up the Earth?
- Why do we depend on the sun in order to live?
- What would life on Earth be like if the sun stopped shining?
- What steps on the wheel did we apply today?

### What to Do at Home
- Ask students to draw a picture of the sun heating the Earth and the heat being trapped by the Earth's atmosphere. This picture should be dated and will be included in the students' log books.

## Handout 11A
# Sunlight Concept Map

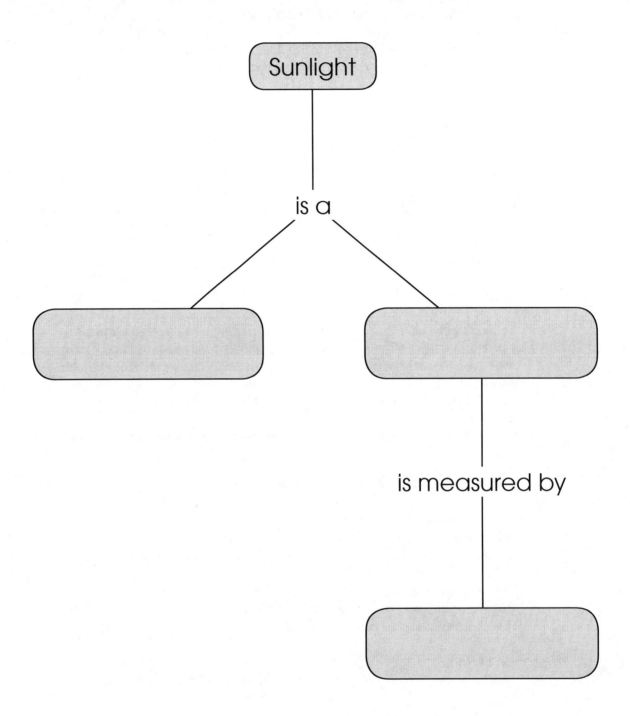

Name:_____ Date:_____

# Diagram of the Greenhouse Effect

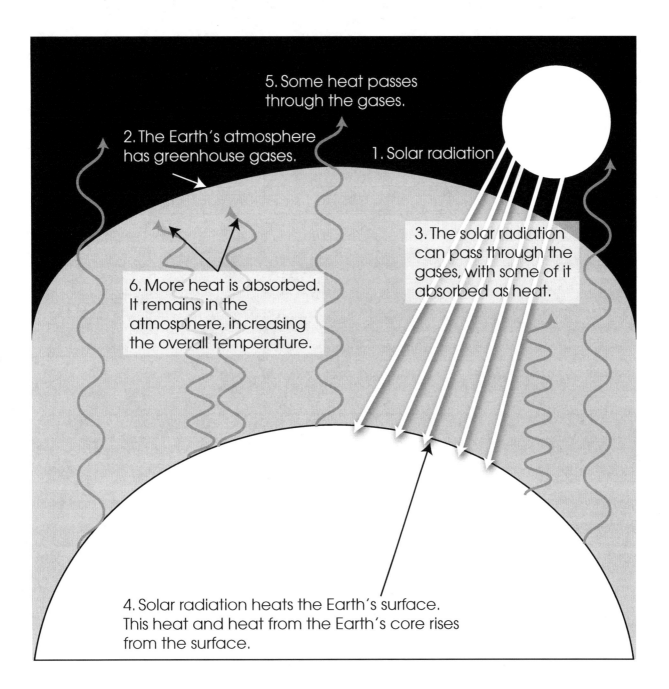

5. Some heat passes through the gases.

2. The Earth's atmosphere has greenhouse gases.

1. Solar radiation

3. The solar radiation can pass through the gases, with some of it absorbed as heat.

6. More heat is absorbed. It remains in the atmosphere, increasing the overall temperature.

4. Solar radiation heats the Earth's surface. This heat and heat from the Earth's core rises from the surface.

Name:_____ Date:_____

# Temperature in a Jar
# Experiment Data Table

| Time | Temperature in the Jar | Temperature Outside the Jar |
|------|------------------------|------------------------------|
|      |                        |                              |
|      |                        |                              |
|      |                        |                              |
|      |                        |                              |
|      |                        |                              |

# Lesson 12:
# It's Getting Hot Down Here!

## Planning the Lesson

### Instructional Purpose
- To analyze how human activity causes an increase in the Earth's temperature (global warming).
- To identify ways to decrease factors that contribute to global warming.

### Instructional Time
- 45 minutes

### Change Concept Generalizations
- Change is everywhere.
- Change is related to time.
- Change can be natural or manmade.
- Change may be random or predictable.

### Key Science Concepts
- Recycling, reusing, and reducing consumption may help to reduce global warming.

### Assessment "Look Fors"
- Students can identify causes of global warming.
- Students can identify ways to reduce global warming.

### Materials/Resources/Equipment
- Lab coat for teacher
- One lab coat (white adult T-shirt or dress shirt) for each student
- Charts or slides of Handouts 12A (Definition of Global Warming), 12B (Things We Can Do to Reduce Global Warming), and 12C (Conservation Concept Map)
- One silhouette of the teacher
- One piece of 12" x 18" white construction paper for each student
- One piece of plain chart paper for each group of 3–4 students
- One shadeless lamp or a large flashlight
- Masking tape
- Markers

## Implementing the Lesson

1. Put on lab coats and review what students learned about the greenhouse effect. Remind students that the heat from the sun is kept close to the Earth because of the Earth's atmosphere. Ask students:
   - How does the Earth stay warm?
   - What would happen if there was no sun?

2. Explain that scientists are concerned because they have noticed that it has been getting hotter on Earth. The temperature has increased by more than 1 degree, which has caused the polar icecaps to melt. The melting ice has caused the sea level to rise.  Scientists call this rise in temperature "global warming" (Handout 12A). Ask students if they have any ideas about why the Earth is getting hotter and encourage them to recall what they have learned about the sun thus far. Ask students:
   - Why do you think the Earth is getting hotter?

3. Explain that humans today have many things that make life easier to live that they did not have a long time ago. Ask students to identify some of the things that people have that make it easier to live now than a long time ago. Students should identify things such as cars, the light bulb, and so forth.

4. Explain that all of these things are conveniences that need energy to run and explain that energy creates heat. To illustrate this point, ask students to run in place for a while and to notice what happens when they run. Relate how when they run they use energy and the energy heats them up. The same is true of all the conveniences we have: they are creating additional heat on Earth, and the Earth's atmosphere is keeping a lot of this additional heat close to the Earth. Scientists' hypothesize that this might be one reason the temperature has risen and theorize this as global warming.

5. Ask students what they think people can do to reduce global warming and write down student comments on chart paper. Have students compare their list to the list that is included on Handout 12B. Explain the items on the list.

6. Review what has been discussed about the greenhouse effect, global warming, and conservation by engaging small groups of four in creating conservation concept maps on large chart paper. Facilitate small groups in creating the concept map as needed. Allow groups to share their maps with the class and compare and contrast maps to the one on Handout 12C.

7. Show students your own silhouette and ask them what it is and how it is made. Ask students how a silhouette is related to shadows.

8. Tape a piece of white construction paper to the wall; have a student stand sideways in front of the paper. Turn on the flashlight and turn out the lights. Direct the light onto the student to create a silhouette. Have students describe the student's silhouette with the following prompts:
   - What physical characteristics do you see in a silhouette?
   - What physical characteristics can you not see?

9. Model how to outline the student's silhouette. Turn on the lights.

10. Cut out the silhouette and hold up the image next to the student. Ask students:
    - How is the silhouette like _____?
    - How is it different?
    - How do you know that this is a silhouette of _____?

11. Explain that you are going to create a silhouette of each child. While you are creating the silhouettes, each student is going to draw a picture showing one thing that they can do to reduce global warming. This picture will be glued to their silhouette to let others know what each student plans to do.

12. Pass out pieces of drawing paper a little smaller than the silhouettes and allow students to write down their commitments and illustrate them.

## Concluding and Extending the Lesson

### Concluding Questions and/or Actions
- How have people caused global warming?
- Describe whether you think global warming is a good or bad thing.
- Why is it important to stop global warming?
- How does the creation of shadows help reduce global warming?
- Display student drawings with their silhouettes.

### What to Do at Home
- Ask students to identify ways they can reduce the use of energy in their homes.

# Definition of Global Warming

**Global Warming . . .**

An average increase in the Earth's temperature, which in turn causes changes in climate.

Global warming may cause:
- Changes in rainfall.
- A rise in the sea level.
- Changes in wildlife, plants, and people.

# Things We Can Do To Reduce Global Warming

- Use less gas.
  - Walk more.
  - Carpool with others.
  - Use cars with smaller engines.

- Use less energy in our homes.
  - Turn off lights when not in use.
  - Reduce the heat temperature in our homes in the winter.
  - Reduce the use of air conditioners in our homes during the summer.
  - Use more insulation in our homes.
  - Keep our doors and windows closed when using air conditioners or heaters.

- Reuse and recycle.

- Plant trees.

# Conservation Concept Map

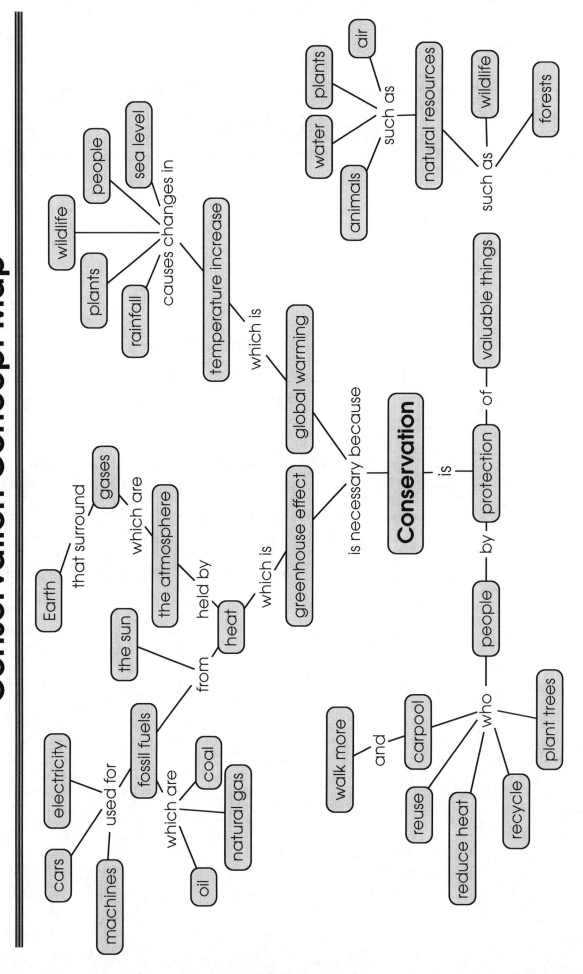

# Lesson 13:
# Shining With Shadows

## Planning the Lesson

### Instructional Purpose
- To celebrate what has been learned about the sun and shadows, change, and scientific investigation by creating shadow figures using manmade and natural light sources.

### Instructional Time
- 45 minutes

### Change Concept Generalizations
- Change is everywhere.
- Change is related to time.
- Change can be natural or manmade.
- Change may be random or predictable.

### Key Science Concepts
- Shadows can occur whenever light is present.
- Shadows can be produced when light is blocked.
- Changes in the sun and shadows can be observed and measured.
- The sun is a natural source of heat and light.
- Natural resources help humans.
- Shadows occur in nature when light is blocked by an object.
- Day and night are caused by the rotation of the Earth.
- Recycling, reusing, and reducing consumption may help to reduce global warming.

### Scientific Investigation Skills and Processes
- Make observations.
- Ask questions.
- Learn more.
- Design and conduct an experiment.
- Create meaning.
- Tell others what was found.

### Assessment "Look Fors"
- Students can apply the change generalizations to review their study of the sun, shadows, and conservation.
- Students can apply knowledge of shadows to create and change shadow figures.
- Students can distinguish between natural and manmade light sources.
- Students can hypothesize about or predict shadows.
- Students can describe the process of scientific investigation.

### Materials/Resources/Equipment
- Lab coat for teacher
- One lab coat (white adult T-shirt or dress shirt) for each student

- Shadow Figure Templates (Handout 13A)
- Directions for Creating Shadow Figures (Handout 13B)
- Copies of Handout 13C (What We Learned From How the Sun Makes Our Day; one per pair of students)
- One badge for each student created from Handout 13D (Official Sun and Shadow Investigator Badge)
- Stage or large space that can be darkened and has a large wall space
- One or two bright spotlights

## Implementing the Lesson

1. Go to a stage area or cafeteria that can be darkened. Ask students if they have observed shadows at night in their home. Use the following questions as prompts:
   - What kinds of objects created shadows in your home?
   - What was the light source that created the shadows?
   - Was the light source natural or manmade?

2. Inform students that they will be creating different shadow shapes on the wall with their hands. Tell them that this is sometimes called "shadow play." Ask students:
   - Have you ever done shadow play in your own home?
   - What light source did you use?
   - How can shadows sometimes fool you to believe an object is something that it's not?
   - What "natural" light source creates shadows at night?

3. Ask students to find their own space on the stage. Show students how they can make their own shadow figures. Turn on a spotlight and turn out the lights. Show the students one shadow animal picture at a time using Handout 13A. Ask students if they can create the shadow animal. Then allow students to create their own shadow animals. If desired, once students have created their own animals, demonstrate how to make several "shadow animals" by following the directions on Handout 13B.

4. Reinforce how distance from the light source affects the shadow's size. Ask students:
   - How can you make your shadow animal smaller?
   - How can you make your shadow animal larger?

5. Ask students to predict if they can create the shadow animals outside, then ask students:
   - Why did you make this prediction?
   - What light source might produce the shadow animals outside?
   - Is this a natural or a manmade light source?

6. Go outside and allow students to attempt to create shadow animals outside and determine whether their prediction is correct. Discuss the following:
   - Tell me why you could/could not create shadow animals outside.
   - Which light source created the best shadow animal? Why?
   - Was the light source natural or manmade?

7. Ask students to sit in a circle. While they are getting in the circle, ask students to think of something that they have learned about the sun and shadows, change, and scientific investigation.
8. Allow students to discuss with a partner what they have learned. If desired, student pairs can use Handout 13C to draw or write down at least one thing learned about: (a) the sun and shadows, (b) change, and (c) scientific investigation. Prompt partners to choose one thing to share with the class concerning what they learned about the sun and shadows, change, and scientific investigation.

## Concluding and Extending the Lesson

### Concluding Questions and/or Actions
- How do scientists conduct an investigation?
- How does the sun cause changes on Earth?
- How is time related to the sun?
- How can we use the sun to predict change?
- Describe whether the sun is helpful to people.
- Provide each student with a picture that represents some unit concept. Ask the students to work together to put the pictures together in a concept map. Help them to make links to build a class concept map, adding words when needed.
- Proclaim that the students are now official scientific investigation sun and shadow experts and pass out Official Sun and Shadow Investigator badges (Handout 13D).

### What to Do at Home
- Allow the students to wear their investigator badges home and encourage them to tell their families what they learned about sun and shadows. Encourage the students to make "shadow animals" at home. Send home directions for making "shadow animals" (Handout 13B).

Name:_____ Date:_____

# Shadow Templates

# Making Shadow Animals

**Bird:**
- Put your hands in front of you, palms up.
- Lay your right wrist on top of your left wrist.
- Link your thumbs together.
- Bring your hands toward you so that your thumbs are pointing toward the ceiling.
- To make the bird fly, bend all of your fingers together back and forth. The bird's wings will appear to flap.

**Dog:**
- Put your hands out in front of you.
- Put your hands together, so that your palms are touching each other.
- To show the dog barking, keep your fingers together and move your pinkies up and down.
- To make the dog's ears, cross your thumbs and make a V.

**Rabbit:**
- Put one hand in front of your face so that you are looking at the palm of your hand.
- To make the rabbit's ears, make a "V" using your index and middle fingers.
- To make the rabbit's head, turn your hand to the side and touch your pinky and your ring finger to the top of your thumb.

**Swan:**
- To make the body of the swan, bend your right arm.
- To make the beak, put your fingers and thumb together on your right hand.
- To make swan's feathers, lay your left wrist where you bent your right arm to make the swan.
- Point the fingers of your left hand toward the ceiling and spread them apart.

Adapted from Zoom (n.d.).

Name:_____ Date:_____

# What We Learned From How the Sun Makes Our Day

What we learned about the sun and shadows:

_____

_____

_____

What we learned about change:

_____

_____

_____

What we learned about scientific investigation:

_____

_____

_____

# Official Sun and Shadow Investigator Badge

Official Sun and Shadow Investigator

Official Sun and Shadow Investigator

Official Sun and Shadow Investigator

Official Sun and Shadow Investigator

Official Sun and Shadow Investigator

Official Sun and Shadow Investigator

# Postassessment Directions
# for the Teacher

## Planning the Lesson

### Instructional Purpose
- To assess student knowledge of the concept of change, student understanding of content about sun and shade, and student skills in the scientific process.

### Instructional Time
- Macroconcept assessment: 30 minutes
- Content assessment: 30 minutes
- Scientific process assessment: 20 minutes

### Materials/Resources/Equipment
- Copies of Postassessment for Change Concept, Incomplete Animals Concept Map, and Word Bank for Animals Concept Map for each student
- Postassessment for Key Science Concepts, Rubric 1 (Scoring Rubric for Change Concept; see p. 28), Preteaching for Key Science Concepts Postassessment, Sample Concept Map, Rubric 2 (Scoring Rubric for Content Assessment; see p. 33), and Rubric 3 (Scoring Rubric for Scientific Process; see p. 40) for your use
- Copies of Does Sand Dissolve in Water?, What Materials Will You Need?, How Would You Conduct Your Experiment?, What Does This Table Show?, and What Will Dissolve? handouts for the Postassessment for the Scientific Process for each student
- Pencils
- Large chart paper
- Drawing paper for each student

## Implementing the Lesson

1. Administer only *one* postassessment per day.
2. Give each student a copy of the postassessments to complete in the order noted above. The assessments should take no more than 80 minutes in all.
3. Explain that the assessment will be used to see how much students have learned during the unit.

## Scoring
- Use the rubrics contained in the preassessment sections for concept, scientific process, and content. Sample exemplar responses are provided after each postassessment.

Name:_____ Date:_____

# Postassessment for Change Concept

1. What is change? In each box, draw a picture or write a word for something that changes.

| | |
|---|---|
| | |
| | |
| | |
| | |

2. Draw a picture of something in your life that changes, and show how it changes. Include as many details as you can.

3. Draw five ways a tree could change or be changed.

# Postassessment for Key Science Concepts

**Directions to Teacher:** Read the following paragraph to the students.

Today I would like you to think about all the things you know about sun and shadows. Think about the words you would use and the pictures you could draw to make a concept map. Think about the connections you can make. On your concept map paper, draw in pictures and words that you know about sun and shadows. You will be drawing a concept map similar to the ones you have done before. Look at the word bank and the concept map. You will use some of the word bank words to fill in the parts of the concept map. Some words are just extras that you won't need. Remember, a concept map is used to tell what we know and to make connections. Today's question is: "Tell me everything you know about sun and shadows."

## For Kindergarten Students

Direct students to use the word bank to complete the assessment. Students also may use other responses that they come up with on their own. Tell students to draw a picture or write the word or letter for their responses in the appropriate blanks. Each correct response earns one point. Students may enter the word *or* just the letter corresponding to the word *or* come up with their own word.

## For First-Grade Students

Direct students to complete the assessment with appropriate words, pictures, or their own choices of words. Each correct response earns one point.

# Incomplete Shadows Concept Map

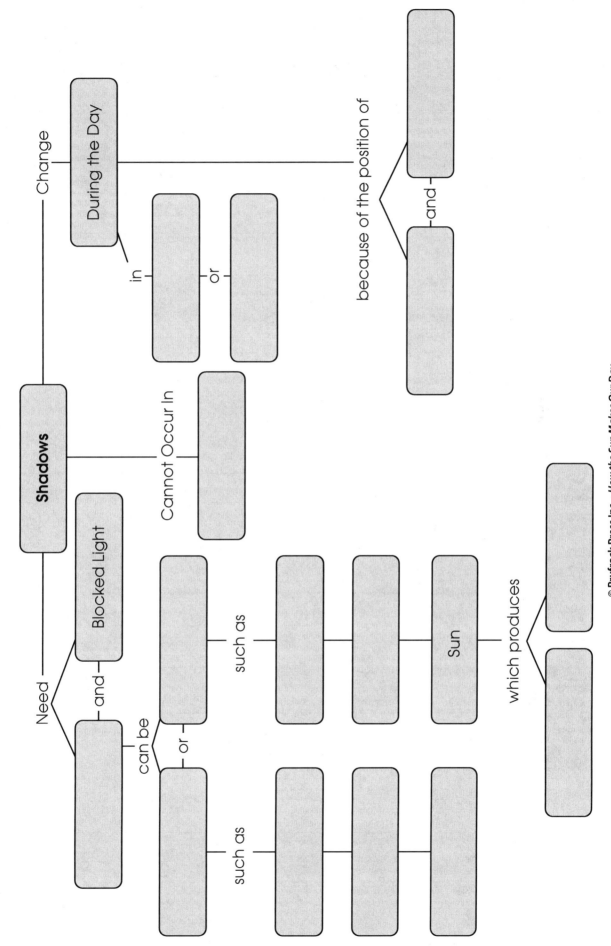

# Preassessment for Key Science Concepts
## Word Bank for Shadows Concept Map

| | | | | | |
|---|---|---|---|---|---|
| **A** Darkness | **B** Dust | **C** Light source | **D** Heat | **E** Shade | **F** Air | **G** Water |
| **H** Tomorrow | **I** Natural | **J** Black | **K** Shadow | **L** Manmade | **M** Rain | **N** Darkness |
| **O** Glow Stick | **P** Light bulb | **Q** Moonlight | **R** Fire | **S** Flashlight | **T** Star light | **U** Headlight |
| **V** Rain | **W** Light | **X** Cold | **Y** Heat | **Z** Pollution | **Aa** Shape | **Bb** Darkness |
| **Cc** Outside | **Dd** Darkness | **Ee** Winter | **Ff** Daylight | **Gg** Water | **Hh** Inside | **Ii** March |
| **Jj** Color | **Kk** Temperature | **Ll** Shape | **Mm** Texture | **Nn** Weight | **Oo** Size | **Pp** Salt |
| **Qq** Stars | **Rr** Moon | **Ss** Meteor | **Tt** Earth | **Uu** Sun | **Vv** Rock | **Ww** Atmosphere |

| | |
|---|---|
| **Shadows need** | |
| **Can be** | |
| **Such as** | |
| **Sun produces** | |
| **Cannot occur in** | |
| **Shadows change in** | |
| **Because of the position of** | |

# Postassessment for the Scientific Process

1. Assess students in groups of 4 to 6.
2. Tell students they are going to think like scientists. Say to students, "I have a scientific question for you: Does sand dissolve in water? You are going to think about whether or not sand dissolves in water. We will work together to look at some pictures and select an answer to some questions about an experiment to find out if sand dissolves in water."
3. Pass out the packet of assessment record sheets on pp. 118–122. Ask students to look at the first sheet (Does Sand Dissolve in Water?). Ask them to write their name on the paper. Direct them to think about the two pictures and make a prediction about whether or not sand dissolves in water. Tell students to put an X in the box under the picture that shows their prediction—sand does not dissolve in water or sand does dissolve in water.
   Picture choices are:
   a. Clear container with water and sand on the bottom
   b. Clear container with water and no sand on the bottom

4. Ask students to think about what materials they will need for their experiment. Look at the What Materials Will You Need? handout (the one that shows some materials that could be used). Ask students to put an X under each picture that shows a material that will be used in the experiment.
   Picture choices are:
   a. Clear container
   b. Spoon
   c. Sand
   d. Salt
   e. Water
   f. Milk

5. Present each student with a set of four cards showing pictures of the steps in the experiment (see the How Would You Conduct the Experiment? handout). Tell the students to select the pictures that show the steps they would take for the experiment. Picture choices are (1) gathering the materials, (2) pouring in water, (3) pouring in sand, (4) stirring the mixture. Instruct students to put the steps they selected in the correct order—which comes first, second, etc. Check to see each student's response and record.
6. Ask students to look at the table on the What Does This Table Show? handout and decide whether it shows that sand dissolves in water or salt does not dissolve in water. Students should put an X in the correct box.
7. Ask students to look at the handout, What Will Dissolve?, with pictures of various materials. The materials are: leaf, twig, salt, JELL-O, crayon, sugar, rock, oatmeal. Direct students to think about things that probably dissolve in water and to place an X in each box under a picture that shows something that will dissolve. Which of these materials will dissolve?

Name:_____ Date:_____

# Does Sand Dissolve in Water?

Does sand dissolve in water? Put an X in the box that matches your prediction.

☐

☐

Name:_____ Date:_____

# What Materials Will You Need?

What materials do you need to conduct your experiment? Put an X in the box of each material you would use.

# How Would You Conduct Your Experiment?

Cut out the pictures below and place them in order of the steps of the water and sand experiment.

Name:_____ Date:_____

# What Does This Table Show?

Did the sand dissolve in water?

| | |
|---|---|
| Cassidy | No |
| Lowell | No |
| Sandy | No |
| Adrian | No |
| Leslie | No |
| Lincoln | No |
| Jonah | No |
| Chwee | No |
| Sun | No |

___ Yes, the sand dissolved in water.

___ No, the sand did not dissolve in water.

# What Will Dissolve?

Put an X in the box below each picture that shows something that will dissolve in water.

□

□

□

□

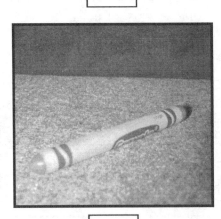

□

□

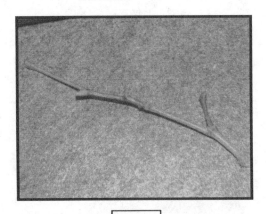

□

□

# Appendix A
# Concept Paper on Change

By Beverly T. Sher, Ph.D.

This paper was adapted from: Sher, B. T. (2004). Change. In J. L. VanTassel-Baska (Ed.), *Science key concepts* (pp. 31–35). Williamsburg, VA: Center for Gifted Education, The College of William and Mary.

We live in a changing world. Change and the absence of change are important features of both scientific and nonscientific processes. Change can occur in simple, predictable ways: Winter gradually gives way to spring, water evaporates from puddles after the rain ends, the sun rises and sets, we (well, most of us, anyway) change from a state of sleep at night to being awake in the daytime. It also can occur in more complicated and unpredictable ways: Hemlines rise and fall apparently randomly, the stock market gyrates, mutations resulting in changed organisms occur, the weather changes. It can also fail to occur: A bottle of root beer in the pantry, when opened, contains the same amount of liquid that it had months earlier at the bottling plant; healthy people maintain roughly the same body temperature at all times (with small, cyclic, daily variations); a rock formation photographed a year ago has the same contours now as it did then. In this concept paper, we will explore the concept of change and the related concept of equilibrium.

There are four general patterns of change. They include:

1. Steady changes: changes that occur at a characteristic rate.
2. Cyclic changes: changes that repeat in cycles.
3. Random changes: changes that occur irregularly, unpredictably, and in a way that is mathematically random.
4. Chaotic changes: changes that appear random and irregular on the surface, but are in fact predictable (in principle).

The first type of change is steady change. Change of this sort occurs at a predictable rate. For example, radioactive decay follows a predictable exponential curve. The number of undecayed atoms remaining after a given time in a radioactive sample can be simply calculated if one knows the half-life of the element involved. For example, half of the atoms in any sample will decay in 14.3 days. Similarly, the distance traveled by a car traveling at 55 miles an hour can be simply calculated for any time after the car leaves (assuming it hasn't run out of gas). Another familiar nonscientific example of steady change would be the steady growth of the balance in an untouched savings account: The rules of compound interest acting on the original balance produce a predictable growth in the daily balance of the account.

The second type of change, cyclic change, frequently is found in nature. A partial list of scientifically interesting cycles would include the phases of the moon, the sunspot cycle, the tides, daily cyclic changes in the levels of hormones in the human body, the sleep-wake cycle in animals, and so on. Some of these examples are familiar to nonscientists as well: We all expect the sun to rise in the east and set in the west once a day, and monthly variations in hormone levels have manifestations that are familiar to almost every female human being over the age of about 13. Other familiar cycles include the credit card billing cycle and the annual recurrence of events such as Christmas, Easter, and fund drives on public television.

The third type of change, random change, also is common in nature. Scientific examples would include the occurrence of spontaneous mutations in genes and the radioactive decay of individual atoms. Nobody can predict when a particular gene in a particular organism will undergo mutation, and nobody can tell by looking at a radioactive atom when it will decay. Interestingly enough, though, these processes that are random at the level of the individual gene or atom have definable rates when one looks at all of the genes in a population of animals (the mutation rate) or all of the radioactive atoms in a sample (the half-life). A similar, nonscientific, example would be winning the lottery. Winning the lottery is a random event. Beforehand, nobody can predict who will win; yet the odds of winning are predictable. Again, this is a process that is unpredictable at the individual level but totally predictable at the level of a population of individuals.

One of the most exciting developments in science in the 1980s was the understanding of chaotic change. Chaos occurs when a system obeys completely predictable behavior (i.e., given the exact state of a system at one time, one can determine its exact state at a future time), but our intrinsic lack of knowledge of its initial state causes its future behavior to appear random. Consider the motion of an asteroid, for example. If you knew the exact position and velocity of an asteroid, you could determine its exact position and velocity at any time in the future. However, a small uncertainty (such as a one millimeter uncertainty in its position) will eventually lead to a huge uncertainty in the future. The position of the asteroid in the future will not be determinable; that is, it will appear random. Similarly, if the location of all of the atoms of our atmosphere were perfectly known at one particular time, the weather could be predicted far into the future. The fact that we don't know those locations exactly (e.g., a butterfly flapping its wings in China will disturb some of the atoms) will lead to huge uncertainties in weather prediction; thus, we will likely never be able to predict the weather very far in advance. It might seem that it is difficult to differentiate between random change and chaotic change, but there are very precise mathematical relations followed by chaotic systems. One of the main realizations of the 1980s was that many systems previously thought to be random, such as water turbulence, weather phenomena, and even cardiac ventricular fibrillation, are in fact chaotic. A good nonscientific example of a chaotic process is the stock market's behavior.

Some systems are characterized not by change but by lack of change. These systems are said to be in equilibrium. The unopened bottle of soda on the shelf in the pantry illustrates this concept in several ways. First, it is static, at rest. All of the outside forces acting on it are balanced: Gravity pulling downward on it is balanced by the force that the shelf exerts to hold it up. Second, the amount of water in it is the same as the amount of water placed in it at the bottling plant. The water in the root beer is not static, however, but is in a state of dynamic equilibrium between two phases: water vapor in the little air space in the neck of the bottle and liquid water in the soda below. The important thing that allows this system to remain in equilibrium is that the bottle is closed. When it is closed, the average number of water molecules that evaporate and leave the liquid phase is exactly balanced by the average number of water molecules condensing from the vapor phase into the liquid phase. Once the bottle is opened, this equilibrium vanishes: Water molecules in the vapor phase can and do escape out the neck of the bottle and the water in the bottle will eventually evaporate. In dynamic equilibrium, therefore, a seeming lack of change reflects balanced processes of change occurring within a system.

The state of dynamic equilibrium that exists in a closed root beer bottle does not depend on any outside forces for its maintenance. Other examples of lack of change, though, represent the interposition of regulatory forces on the system. A simple example of such a system is the thermostat-house system. When the temperature in the house drops below a predetermined level, the sensor in the thermostat notices this and causes the furnace to heat the house. Once the house is warm again, the sensor in the thermostat causes the furnace to shut off. The maintenance of a constant temperature in the house is thus dependent on the regulatory behavior of the sensor. Feedback from the sensor keeps the system stable.

Another, more complicated example of regulated constancy is homeostasis: the maintenance of physical stability within an organism. In humans, for example, everything from our body temperature to the concentrations of different ions in our bloodstream remains fairly constant. This reflects tight control exerted by the cells of our body over these systems: regulation that requires constant sensing of the current state of affairs and compensation for changes that occur as we move, eat, sleep, and do all of the other things that humans do. One example of the mechanisms involved in homeostasis is the action of insulin and its function in regulating blood sugar levels. As a carbohydrate-rich meal begins to be absorbed by the body, the amount of glucose in the bloodstream begins to rise. In response to this, insulin is secreted by the pancreas into the bloodstream. Insulin stimulates the liver to take up extra sugar and store it in the form of glycogen (a starch-like substance); it increases the uptake of sugar by muscle cells and its conversion into glycogen; it inhibits the liver from producing glucose from its glycogen stores; and it stimulates muscle and liver cells to "burn" glucose for energy at a more rapid rate. These activities reduce the amount of glucose in the bloodstream, insulin secretion by the pancreas drops, and things are back to normal. The control of blood sugar levels by the body is complicated and requires a great deal of coordination among the different cells of the body.

## Rationale for Teaching the Concept

Change is an inescapable feature of both scientific and nonscientific systems; indeed, it is often the most interesting feature of either kind of system. In science, for example, the study of developmental biology is concerned entirely with the mechanisms behind the amazing changes that occur as an organism develops from seed or fertilized egg into its mature form; meteorology concerns itself with atmospheric changes; and much of geology involves the study of the changes that have occurred since the Earth was formed. Outside of science, the daily changes in the stock market are important to millions of investors; changes in the weather matter to essentially everyone; and the changes that occur as a baby grows into an adult fascinate parents, grandparents, and teachers alike. An understanding of the basic types of change, as well as of the concept of equilibrium, is useful for anyone.

## Suggested Applications

Many areas of science involve change. Below is a very partial list of suggestions for areas that could be used in illustrating change, equilibrium, and regulation.

### Steady Change

Simple physical changes:
- Temperature change in water as it is heated (and what do you see at the freezing and boiling points?)
- Titration of an acid with a base; watch the pH change
- Rates of random change (mutation formation, radioactive decay)

### Cyclic Change

- Astronomical phenomena (phases of the moon, seasons, changes in day length over the course of the year, behavior of the tides)
- Biological cycles: life cycles, sleep-wake cycle, opening and closing of flowers in plants over the course of the day, the turning of sunflowers to follow the sun, the menstrual cycle

### Random Change

- Radioactive decay
- Spontaneous mutation formation in microbes and man
- Study of probability and statistics

### Chaotic Change

As discussed above, chaotic change is change that could in principle be predicted but, in fact, is unpredictable because of the large numbers of variables involved and uncertainty in measuring starting conditions. Younger children probably have enough difficulty learning that change can be predicted (steady change, cyclic change, rates of random change); introducing chaos at the same time might be confusing. For older children (grades 6–8 or so), the best introduction to chaos would probably be to play with a calculator or computer: Once they have seen the concept in this abstract way, they'll be able to see it in more concrete ways (one of the few cases where hands-on experimentation may *not* be the best way to introduce a new concept!).

### Feedback, Control, and Regulation

- Electronics: study systems like thermostats
- Physiology (human and animal)

# Appendix B
# Teaching Models

## Introduction to the Teaching Models

Several teaching models are incorporated into the Project Clarion units. These models ensure emphasis on unit outcomes and support student understanding of the concepts and processes that are the focus of each unit. Teachers should become familiar with these models and how to use them before teaching the unit. The models are listed below and outlined in the pages that follow.

1. Frayer Model of Vocabulary Development
2. Taba Model of Concept Development
3. Concept Mapping
4. Wheel of Scientific Investigation and Reasoning

## Frayer Model of Vocabulary Development

The Frayer Model (Frayer, Frederick, & Klausmeier, 1969) provides students with a graphic organizer that asks them to think about and describe the meaning of a word or concept. This process enables them to strengthen their understanding of vocabulary words. Through the model, students are required to consider the important characteristics of the word and to provide examples and nonexamples of the concept. This model has similarities to the Taba Model of Concept Development (1962).

In introducing the Frayer Model to your students, demonstrate its use on large chart paper. Begin with a word all students know, such as rock, umbrella, or shoe, placing it on the graphic model. First, ask the students to define the word in their own words. Record a definition that represents their common knowledge. Next, ask students to give specific characteristics of the word/concept or facts they know about it. Record these ideas. Then ask students to offer examples of the idea and then nonexamples to finish the graphic (see Figure B1).

Another way to use the Frayer Model is to provide students with examples and nonexamples and ask them to consider what word or concept is being analyzed. You can provide similar exercises by filling in some portions of the graphic and asking students to complete the remaining sections.

As students share ideas, note the level of understanding of the group and of individual students. As the unit is taught, certain vocabulary words may need this type of expanded thinking to support student readiness for using the vocabulary in the science activities. You may want students to maintain individual notebooks of words so that they can refer back to them in their work.

## Taba Model of Concept Development

Each Project Clarion unit supports the development of a specific macroconcept (change or systems). The concept development model, based upon the work of Hilda Taba (1962), supports student learning of the macroconcept. The model involves both inductive and deductive reasoning processes. Used as an early lesson in the unit, the model focuses on the creation of generalizations about the macroconcept from a student-derived list of created concept examples. The model includes a series

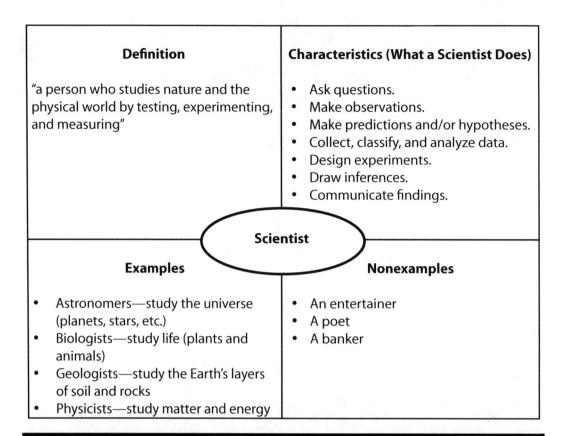

| Definition | Characteristics (What a Scientist Does) |
|---|---|
| "a person who studies nature and the physical world by testing, experimenting, and measuring" | • Ask questions.<br>• Make observations.<br>• Make predictions and/or hypotheses.<br>• Collect, classify, and analyze data.<br>• Design experiments.<br>• Draw inferences.<br>• Communicate findings. |
| Examples | Nonexamples |
| • Astronomers—study the universe (planets, stars, etc.)<br>• Biologists—study life (plants and animals)<br>• Geologists—study the Earth's layers of soil and rocks<br>• Physicists—study matter and energy | • An entertainer<br>• A poet<br>• A banker |

**Scientist**

**Figure B1.** Completed graphic organizer for Frayer Model.

of steps, in which each step involves student participation. Students begin with a broad concept, determine specific examples of the broad concept, create appropriate categorization systems, cite nonexamples of the concept, establish generalizations based on their understanding, and then apply the generalizations to their readings and other situations.

The model generally is most effective when small groups of students work through each step, with whole-class debriefing following each stage of the process. However, with primary-age students, additional teacher guidance may be necessary, especially for the later stages of the model. The steps of the model are outlined below, using the unit concept of change.

1. Students generate examples of the concept of change, derived from their own understanding and experiences with change in the world. Teachers should encourage students to provide at least 15–20 examples; a class list may be created out of the small-group lists to lengthen the set of changes students have to work with.

2. Students then group their changes into categories. This process allows students to search for interrelatedness and to organize their thinking. It often is helpful to have individual examples written on cards so that the categorization may occur physically as well as mentally or in writing. Students should then explain their reasoning for their categorization system and seek clarification from each other as a whole group. Teachers should ensure that all examples have been accounted for in the categorization system established.

3. Students then generate a list of nonexamples of the concept of change. Teachers may begin this step with the direction, "Now list examples of things that *do not change*." Encourage students to think carefully about their

nonexamples and discuss ideas within their groups. Each group should list five to six nonexamples.

4. The students next determine generalizations about the concept of change, using their lists of examples, categories, and nonexamples. Teachers should then share the unit generalizations and relate valid student generalizations to the unit list. Both lists should be posted in the room throughout the course of the unit.

5. During the unit, students are asked to identify specific examples of the generalizations from their own readings, or to describe how the concept applies to a given situation about which they have read. Students also are asked to apply the generalizations to their own writings and their own lives. Several lessons employ a chart that lists several of the generalizations and asks students to supply examples specifically related to the reading or activity of that lesson.

## Concept Mapping

A concept map is a graphic representation of one's knowledge on a particular topic. Concept maps support learning, teaching, and evaluation (Novak & Gowin, 1984). Students clarify and extend their own thinking about a topic. Teachers find concept mapping useful for envisioning the scope of a lesson or unit. They also use student-developed concept maps as a way of measuring their progress. Meaningful concept maps often begin with a particular question (focus question) about a topic, event, or object.

Concept maps were developed in 1972 by Dr. Joseph Novak at Cornell University as part of his research about young children's understanding of science concepts. Students were interviewed by researchers who recorded their responses. The researchers sought an effective way to identify changes in students' understanding over time. Novak and his research colleagues began to represent the students' conceptual understanding in concept maps because learning takes place through the assimilation of new concepts and propositions into existing conceptual and propositional frameworks.

Concept maps show concepts and relationships between them. (See the sample concept map in Figure B2.) The concepts are contained within boxes or oval shapes and the connections between concepts are represented by lines with linking words.

Concepts are the students' perceived ideas generalized from particular experiences. Sometimes the concepts placed on the map may contain more than one word. Words placed on the line link words or phrases. The propositions contain two or more concepts connected by linking words or phrases to form a meaningful statement.

The youngest students may view and develop concept maps making basic connections. They may begin with two concepts joined by a linking word. These "sentences" (propositions) become the building blocks for concept maps. Older students may begin to make multiple connections immediately as they develop their maps.

As students map their knowledge base, they begin to represent their conceptual understanding in a hierarchical manner. The broadest, most inclusive concepts often are found at the top of a concept map. More specific concepts and examples then follow.

Each Project Clarion unit contains an overview concept map, showing the essential knowledge included in the lessons and the connections students should be able to make as a result of their experiences within the unit. This overview may be useful as a classroom poster that the teacher and students may refer to throughout the unit.

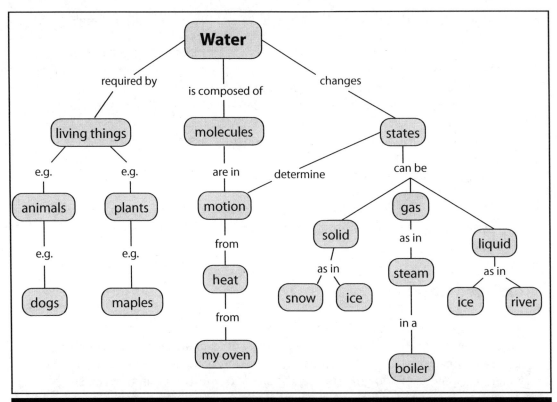

**Figure B2.** A concept map showing a student's understanding of water.

*Note.* Adapted from Novak and Gowin (1984).

## Strategies to Prepare Students for Concept Mapping

The following strategies can be incorporated to help prepare your students for concept mapping activities (Novak & Gowin, 1984).

### What Do Words Mean?
1. Ask students to picture in their minds some common words (e.g., water, tree, door, box, pencil, dog). Start with "object" words, saying them one at a time, allowing time for students to picture each of them.
2. Create a class list of object words, asking students to name other objects they can picture in their minds to add to the list.
3. Next, create a list of event words (e.g., jumping, running, eating). Ask students to envision each of these in their minds and encourage them to contribute to the class list of event words.
4. Give students a few words that are likely to be unfamiliar to most of them, asking if they can see a picture in their mind. These words should be short (e.g., data, cell, prey, inertia). You might include a few simple words in another language. Ask students if they have any mind pictures.
5. Discuss the fact that words are useful to us because they convey meaning. This only happens when people can form a picture in their mind that represents the meaning they connect with the word.

### What Is a Concept?
1. Introduce the word *concept* and explain that concept is the word we use to mean some kind of object or event we can picture in our mind. Refer back to the word lists previously developed as you discuss the word and ask if these

are concepts. Can students see a picture in their mind for each of them? Let students know that when they come upon a word they do not know well enough to form a picture, they will just need to learn the concept associated with that new word.

2. Provide each table with picture cards and ask students to take turns at their table naming some of the concepts included in the card.

### What Are Linking Words?

1. Prepare a list of words such as *the, is, are, when, that, then*. Ask students if they can see a picture in their mind for each of these words. Explain that these are not concept words. These are linking words we use when we speak or write to link concept words together into sentences that have special meaning. Ask students if they have any words to add to the list. Label the list "Linking Words."

2. Hold up two picture cards (sky and blue) and give students a sample sentence ("The sky is blue.") Ask students to tell you the concept words and the linking words in your sentence. Give another example.

3. Give each pair of students a few picture cards. Ask the students to work with partners to pick up two cards and then develop a sentence that links the two cards. They should take turns, with one partner making the sentence and the other identifying the concepts and the linking words. Ask them to repeat this a few times and then have several partners share their sentences.

4. Explain to students that it is easy to make up sentences and to read sentences where the printed labels (words) are familiar to them. Explain that reading and writing sentences is like making a link between two things (concepts) they already know. Practice this idea during reading time, asking students to find a sentence and analyze it for concepts and linking words.

## Wheel of Scientific Investigation and Reasoning

All scientists work to improve our knowledge and understanding of the world. In the process of scientific inquiry, scientists connect evidence with logical reasoning. Scientists also apply their imaginations as they devise hypotheses and explanations that make sense of the evidence. Students can strengthen their understanding of particular science topics through investigations that cause them to employ evidence gathering, logical reasoning, and creativity. The Wheel of Scientific Investigation and Reasoning contains the specific processes involved in scientific inquiry to guide students' thinking and actions.

### Make Observations

Scientists make careful observations and try things out. They must describe things as accurately as possible so that they can compare their observations from one time to another and so that they can compare their observations with those of other scientists. Scientists use their observations to form questions for investigation.

### Ask Questions

Scientific investigations usually are initiated through a problem to be solved or a question asked. Selecting just the right question or clearly defining the problem to be addressed is critical to the investigation process.

### Learn More

To clarify their questions, scientists learn more by reviewing bodies of scientific knowledge documented in text and previously conducted investigations. Also, when scientists get conflicting information they make fresh observations and insights that may result in revision of the previously formed question. By learning more, scientists can design and conduct more effective experiments or build upon previously conducted experiments.

### Design and Conduct the Experiment

Scientists use their collection of relevant evidence, their reasoning, and their imagination to develop a hypothesis. Sometimes scientists have more than one possible explanation for the same set of observations and evidence. Often when additional observations and testing are completed, scientists modify current scientific knowledge.

To test out hypotheses, scientists design experiments that will enable them to control conditions so that their results will be reliable. Scientists repeat their experiments, doing it the same way it was done before and expect to get very similar, although not exact, results. It is important to control conditions in order to make comparisons. Scientists sometimes are not sure what will happen because they don't know everything that might be having an effect on the experiment's outcome.

### Create Meaning

Scientists analyze the data that are collected from the experiment to add to the existing body of scientific knowledge. They organize their data using data tables and graphs and then make inferences from the data to draw conclusions about whether their question was answered and the effectiveness of their experiments. Scientists also create meaning by comparing what they found to existing knowledge. The analysis of data often leads to identification of related questions and future experiments.

### Tell Others What Was Found

In the investigation process, scientists often work as a team, sharing findings with each other so that they may benefit from the results. Initially, individual team members complete their own work and draw their own conclusions.

One way to introduce the wheel to students is to provide them with the graphic model (see Figure B3) and ask them to tell one reason why each section of the wheel is important to scientific investigation.

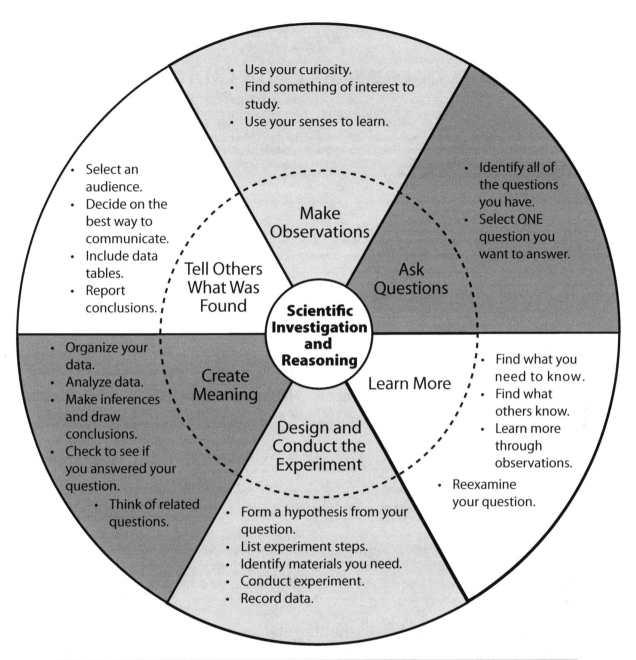

**Figure B3.** Wheel of Scientific Investigation and Reasoning model.

*Note.* Adapted from Kramer (1987).

# Appendix C
# Basic Concepts in Early Childhood

By Bruce A. Bracken, Ph.D., and Elizabeth Crawford

This paper was adapted from: Bracken, B. A., & Crawford, E. (2009). *Basic concepts in early childhood educational standards: A 50 state review*. Manuscript submitted for publication.

This paper presents the authors' conceptualization of basic concepts as the foundation of early childhood knowledge (e.g., Bracken, 1998a). This paper's focus on basic language concepts asserts the importance of empirically supported educational interventions to reinforce systematic acquisition of basic concepts that all children must possess. These basic concepts are the language arts knowledge necessary to explore, comprehend, and discuss topical concepts in all content areas if they are to succeed in early childhood education and beyond. This fact is especially true for children from diverse cultural and linguistic backgrounds, and those with exceptionalities.

The paper provides a comprehensive table of concept knowledge (Table C1) that promotes systematic concept instruction. The table identifies foundational content and conceptual categories, subdomains of knowledge comprised within these categories, and examples of specific concepts, referred to throughout this article as "Bracken concepts" to illustrate the depth and breadth of readiness content revealed in the universe of more than 300 essential basic concepts.

## The Bracken Concepts

When the Bracken Basic Concept Scale (BBCS; Bracken, 1984, 1998b, 2006a, 2006b) was conceived, it was the author's belief that there were some largely unspoken, yet agreed upon, concept-based standards in early childhood education. As this line of work progressed it became clear that there was a previously untapped universal list of essential readiness concepts and concept categories. These school readiness concepts have been shown to be valid predictors of early childhood academic success (Panter, 2000; Panter & Bracken, 2000, in press; Stebbins & McIntosh, 1996; Sterner & McCallum, 1988), cognitive development (Breen, 1985; Howell & Bracken, 1992; McIntosh, Brown, & Ross, 1995; McIntosh, Wayland, Gridley, & Barnes, 1995), language development (Bracken & Cato, 1986; Rhyner & Bracken, 1988); and, they also are ubiquitous within early childhood test directions for early childhood academic and intelligence tests (Bracken, 1986; Bracken & Brown, 2008; Cummings & Nelson, 1980; Flanagan, Alfonso, Kaminer, & Rader, 1995; Kaufman, 1978). Importantly, these concepts can be taught easily, resulting in large educational gains (Wilson, 2004) and their development proceeds along a clear developmental sequence (Bracken, 1988) across both English and Spanish languages (Bracken, et al., 1990; Bracken & Fouad, 1987).

The intent of the Bracken concept list was to identify the universe of basic concepts for parents and teachers so they might more systematically, comprehensively, and effectively teach young children. As such, the Bracken concepts represent one of the first efforts to informally establish early childhood instructional standards. The *Bracken Concept Development Program* (BBCD; Bracken, 1987) was published to provide a direct curricular link between the assessment of children's basic concept knowledge and conceptual instruction. The BCDP presents 19 educationally

# Table C1
# Early Childhood Conceptual Categories

| Concept Category | Subdomain | Concept Examples |
|---|---|---|
| Colors | • Primary Colors<br>• Secondary Colors<br>• Tertiary Colors<br>• Absolutes | • Red, Yellow, Blue<br>• Orange, Green, Purple<br>• Violet, Heather<br>• White, Black |
| Letters | • Recognition<br>  - Uppercase<br>  - Lowercase<br>• Naming<br>  - Uppercase<br>  - Lowercase<br><br>• Letter Sounds<br>• Letter Blend Sounds<br><br>• Letter Production | <br>• Point to M, B, S, D<br>• Point to u, v, c, b<br><br>• Name this letter, W, P, R, E<br>• Name this letter, a, e, g, k<br><br>• What sound does b make?<br>• What sound does ch make?<br><br>• Print the letter X, J, Z |
| Numbers/<br>Counting | • Rote Counting<br>• Place Counting<br><br>• Number Identification<br>  - 0–9<br>  - Double Digits<br>  - Triple Digits<br><br>• Number Naming<br>  - 0–9<br>  - Double Digits<br>  - Triple Digits<br><br>• Number Production<br>• Counting by Sets | • Counting without place value<br>• Counting with one-to-one correspondence<br><br><br>• Point to the 1, 5, 8, 0<br>• Point to the 22, 58, 95<br>• Point to 138, 395, 783<br><br><br>• What is this number? 2, 6, 9<br>• What is this number? 44, 78<br>• What is this number? 234, 783<br><br>• Print the number 6, 33, 245<br>• Count to 100 by 2s, 5s, 10s |
| Size/Comparisons | • Three-Dimensional Size<br>• Two-Dimensional Size<br>  - Vertical<br>  - Horizontal<br><br>• Comparative Sizes | • Big, Large, Small, Little<br><br>• Tall, Short<br>• Long, Short<br><br>• Similar, Same, Different |
| Shapes | • Linear (vertical/horizontal)<br>  - Curvilinear Line<br>  - Diagonal Line<br>  - Angular Line<br><br>• Two-Dimensional Shapes<br>• Three-Dimensional Shapes | • Line, Straight<br>• Curve<br>• Diagonal<br>• Angle<br><br>• Circle, Square, Triangle<br>• Sphere, Cube, Pyramid |
| Direction/Position | • Three-Dimensional Direction<br>• Internal/External<br>• Relative Proximity<br>• Self/Other Perspective<br>• Front/Rear<br>• Specific Locations<br>• Cardinal Directions | • Under, Over, Right, Left<br>• Inside, Outside, Around<br>• Near, Far, Beside<br>• My Right, Your Right, My Left, Your Left<br>• In Front of, Behind, Forward, Backward<br>• Edge, Corner<br>• North, South, East, West |

| Concept Category | Subdomain | Concept Examples |
|---|---|---|
| Self-/Social Awareness | • Affective Feeling<br>• Health/Physical<br>• Gender<br>• Familial Relationships<br>• Age<br>• Mores | • Happy, Sad, Excited<br>• Healthy, Sick, Tired<br>• Boy, Girl, Woman, Man, Male, Female<br>• Mother, Father, Brother<br>• Old, Young<br>• Right, Wrong, Correct |
| Texture/Material | • States of Matter<br>• Textures<br>• Materials<br>• Material Characteristics<br>• Temperatures | • Solid, Liquid, Gas<br>• Rough, Smooth, Sharp<br>• Cloth, Wood, Metal<br>• Wet, Dry, Shiny, Dull<br>• Hot, Cold |
| Quantity | • Part/Whole<br>• Relative Quantity<br>• Volume<br>• Multiples<br>• Comparatives/Superlatives<br>• Fractions<br>• Math Signs/Symbols | • Whole, Part, Piece<br>• Lots, Few, Some, None<br>• Full, Empty<br>• Pair, Double, Triple, Dozen<br>• More, Less, Most, Least<br>• Half, One-Third<br>• +, -, x |
| Time/Sequence | • Mathematical Seriation<br>• Frequency<br>• Natural Occurring Events<br>• Temporal Order of Events<br>• Temporal Absolutes<br>• Scheduling<br>• Speed<br>• Relative Age<br>• Temporal Nuances<br>• Larger Temporal Periods | • First, Second, Third<br>• Once, Twice<br>• Morning, Daytime, Evening<br>• Before, After, Finished<br>• Never, Always<br>• Early, Late, Next, Arriving<br>• Fast, Slow<br>• New, Old, Young, Old<br>• Nearly, Just, Waiting<br>• Days, Weeks, Months, Seasons, Years |

sound and empirically supported principles for teaching basic concepts to young children (see Table C2). The Bracken concept list and instructional principles have become important in early childhood assessment and instruction internationally (Bracken, 1984, 1987, 1998b, 2006a, 2006b) because the BCDP integrates this available knowledge and a comprehensive list of basic language concepts into systematic classroom instruction (Bracken, 1987).

A comprehensive discussion of basic concepts is presented below by conceptual categories to bring uniformity to the teaching of basic concepts.

# Colors

Colors are described as primary, secondary, or tertiary, and often are learned by young children in approximately that order. Primary colors are red, yellow, and blue. These colors are considered primary because no combination of colors is blended to produce a primary color. Secondary colors, on the other hand, are colors that result from blending two primary colors. As such, when the two primary colors yellow and blue are combined, they create the secondary color green; when red and blue are combined, they create purple; and when yellow and red are combined, they form orange. Orange, green, and purple then are secondary colors. When primary colors are blended with secondary colors, tertiary or intermediate colors are created, which vary depending on the proportions of each color added to the admixture (e.g., blue and green combined form the tertiary colors blue-green, heather, aquamarine, teal, and so on depending on the proportions of blue or green added).

# Table C2
# Instructional Principles for Teaching the Bracken Basic Concepts

| | Bracken Instructional Principle |
|---|---|
| 1 | Language, examples, materials, and procedures used to teach concepts should be less complex than the concept being taught. |
| 2 | When concepts occur in pairs (e.g., up, down) or in series (e.g., before, just, after), maximize the meaningfulness of each concept by teaching all relevant concepts during the same lesson. |
| 3 | As much as possible, teach simple concepts, conceptual pairs, and series by using mnemonic strategies that facilitate understanding and enhance memory. |
| 4 | Concept generalizations should be taught initially by instruction with obvious examples of the concept and proceed to less obvious, more extreme examples. This instructional format should be followed with cases in which "nonexamples" are used to teach concept discrimination. Nonexamples should range initially from the apparent to relative nuances in later lessons. |
| 5 | Identify the characteristics that define the concept, distinguish which single dimension or group of characteristics are most salient, and provide instruction that initially emphasizes the most important characteristics, while minimizing the less important or irrelevant dimensions. |
| 6 | Instruction of polar concepts or concepts in a continuum should begin with the positive pole concept. |
| 7 | Concept pairs should be taught so that children identify positive examples as being *the concept* and negative examples (nonexamples) as *not being the concept*. Objects, for example, are either *tall* or *not tall*. |
| 8 | Once the positive pole concept is accurately described as *the concept* or *not the concept*, the child is taught that when it is *not the concept* it is the *negative pole concept* (e.g., if the object is *not tall*, then it is *short*). |
| 9 | When both polar concepts are learned, the teacher continues to display the logic that if it is *not the positive concept*, then it is *the negative concept* and if it is *not the negative concept*, then it is *the positive concept* (e.g., if the object is *not short*, then it is *tall*). |
| 10 | Consider the sequence in which concepts are acquired; the teacher should continually teach and assess to ensure that concept instruction is at the appropriate level. |
| 11 | School instruction should provide parents with a list of concepts and helpful suggestions as to how concepts can best be taught at home. |
| 12 | Conceptual lessons should elicit active participation and allow for multisensory instructional presentations. |
| 13 | Allow for overlearning in concept instruction by incorporating previously learned concepts in the lessons designed to teach new concepts. |
| 14 | Keep concept instructional sessions appropriately brief. |
| 15 | To ensure overlearning of concepts, allow for an adequate review of previously learned concepts before proceeding to new concepts. |
| 16 | Begin instructional sessions at a level that ensures success. Maintain an instructional difficulty level that guarantees continued success. |
| 17 | Structure conceptual instruction sessions so that each has an identifiable beginning and ending and objectives are clear. |
| 18 | Concepts should be taught in familiar situations in order to facilitate generalization. |
| 19 | To ensure a thorough understanding of basic concepts as instruction progresses, sessions should include conceptual combinations that are more complex than the instruction of single concepts. |

*Note.* Adapted from Bracken (1987).

In addition to primary, secondary, and tertiary colors, there are the additional absolute colors of white and black. From a natural beam of light perspective, white is the combination of all primary colors, colors that can be separated into the full color spectrum comprised in a prism array. From an artificial, projected light beam perspective, white is the combination of red, green, and blue. Also from a light beam perspective, black is the total absence of color or as an extension, the absence of light. From a materials perspective, however, white is the absence of any color pigmentation and black is the combination of all colors. As such, white and black are contributors to the lightening or darkening of primary or secondary colors by degree of addition to the color admixture.

In combination, primary and secondary colors with the absolute colors of white and black added are universal colors for all people with normal color vision and should constitute the educational basis for standards in color recognition and naming (Bracken, 1984, 1998b, 2006a, 2006b). Young children should be able to describe objects in terms of color, including the most basic primary and secondary colors, plus white and black.

## Letters

Recognizing and naming the 26 letters of the alphabet appears to be the very foundation upon which reading preliteracy skills are developed. Developmental literature and the difficulty levels achieved among the Bracken concepts concur that children reliably recognize uppercase (i.e., capital) letters before they recognize lowercase letters, and later they are also able to name uppercase before lowercase letters, and later still they are able to reproduce the sounds that individual letters and consonant blends make.

The Bracken concept list includes the prereading concepts to include important phonemic awareness skills and abilities (i.e., letter and initial consonant blend sounds). Ideally, standards, curriculum, and instruction would systematically follow the developmental sequence of recognition followed by expression, including: (1) identifying uppercase letters, (2) identifying lowercase letters, (3) uppercase letter naming, (4) lowercase letter naming, (5) letter-sound production, and (6) initial consonant blend production.

## Numbers/Counting

As with prereading skills, premath and early math skills have a fairly predictable developmental progression. Early on, young children develop a sense of quantity (e.g., more/less) and develop the ability to rote count without a one-to-one number/object correspondence. Later, young children learn to recognize numbers 1–5, followed by 6–9 and zero, and then double-digit numbers. Along the way, young children begin to count to 10 with one-to-one correspondence, and quickly they are on to counting to numbers greater than 100. Later still, young students learn to count by twos, fives, 10s, and so on.

## Sizes/Comparisons

Sizes and comparative knowledge about size can be thought of in a number of ways, including considering objects in terms of their overall, three-dimensional size (e.g., big, small, large, little) or two-dimensional size, which may be depicted as vertical (e.g., tall, short) or horizontal (e.g., short, long), or diagonal. The developmental literature and item difficulty levels on the BBCS-R3 (Bracken, 2006a) generally support the assertion that students first learn concepts related to gross, three-dimensional size (e.g., big, small) before learning concepts related to two-dimensional size (e.g., tall, long). Students must be able to discern similarities and differences between the many attributes or dimensions of objects in our environment, including dimensions of relative size (e.g., same, equal, different),the more basic Bracken concepts of equal and unequal, and concepts in their most basic form (e.g., short), as well as in their comparative and superlative forms (i.e., shorter, shortest). Additional concepts that provide a more complete list of size concepts include unique contexts (e.g., deep/shallow, thin, thick) or employ comparative size language (e.g., same, not the same, equal, unequal, match, exact, similar).

## Shapes

At the most basic level, shapes begin with lines, which may be straight, curvilinear (i.e., curved), or angled. Lines also may run in vertical, horizontal, or diagonal orientations.

Lines may be connected to create a whole object with two-dimensions (e.g., circle, square) or three-dimensions (e.g., sphere, cube). The comprehensive Bracken list includes many concepts such as those that define line nature (e.g., straight, curve, diagonal, angle), as well as a full range of two- and three-dimensional shapes (e.g., diamond, curve, angle, heart, checkmark, column, row, diagonal).

## Direction/Position

Directions and locations (or positions) are relational concepts that describe the relative location or position of objects in space. From an early developmental orientation (i.e., non-perspective-taking orientation), objects are viewed in their locations from the perspective of the child (e.g., right is from the child's right-hand perspective); older children with the ability to take another's perspective can view locations from the orientation of others (e.g., opposing orientation where Sally's right is understood as the student's left). From a basic knowledge point of view, directional concepts are first learned from a self-perspective orientation and then later from another's perspective.

In addition to perspective, directions and position concepts by and large are represented most frequently as prepositions, but they also may include nouns (e.g., edge, corner). Early directional knowledge emphasizes a three-dimensional orientation from a self-perspective, and includes concepts that address vertical (e.g., above, below, up, down, under, over, high, low, top, bottom), horizontal (e.g., right, left, beside, next to, sideways), three-dimensional (e.g., around, through), internal/external (e.g., in, out, inside, outside, between), relative proximity (e.g., near, close, far), and the child's front or rear (e.g., front, back, forward, backward).

The Bracken concept list includes all of the aforementioned concepts plus many other related directional or positional concepts (e.g., falling, rising, together, apart, side, toward, away, apart, joined, together, height, length, opposite, level, space, moving, still, beginning, end, open, closed, on, off, upside down, following, ahead, behind). The Bracken Concept Development Program provides a comprehensive, logical extension of knowledge and a systematic treatment of the given universe of content.

## Self- and Social Awareness

The domain of self- and social awareness includes a wide array of personological and sociological knowledge, including affective feelings, health and physical condition, gender awareness, familial relationships, relative age, and social mores or correctness. As with academic content areas, students' sense of self and developing self-concepts are developmental in nature (Bracken, 1996).

The Bracken concept list includes the most comprehensive collection of concepts and knowledge in the area of self- and social-awareness. The Bracken concepts include conceptual knowledge associated with gender (e.g., male, female, boy, girl), familial relations (e.g., brother, sister, mother, father), age (e.g., old, young), health and physical awareness (e.g., tired, fatigued, rested, healthy, hurt, relaxing, sleepy, sick), affective state (e.g., happy, sad, crying, laughing, smiling, angry, afraid, excited, frowning, worried, curious), and social mores (e.g., right, wrong, correct, easy, difficult).

## Texture/Material

From a developmental perspective, young children from birth begin to learn directly about their environments, including the attributes that define or characterize the objects in their environments. As infants crawl and toddlers toddle about and handle objects, they begin to develop an awareness of different textures (e.g., rough, hard, soft, smooth) and material characteristics or conditions (e.g., heavy, wet, dry, light). Parents begin to teach their children at very early ages the safety concept of hot and by comparison the polar opposite concept of cold. Much later, children begin to learn what the objects in their environments are made of (e.g., wood, metal, glass, cloth) and they relate to the textures and material attributes that are consistent with each material (e.g., wood is hard; metal is heavy; glass is clear or sharp; cloth is soft, or sometimes rough). Finally, children learn about the manmade changing states of objects or materials (e.g., rough wood can be sanded smooth) or natural changing states of objects and materials (e.g., water can be found in various states, depending on temperature [i.e., liquid, solid, gas]). Such a comprehensive consideration and treatment of materials and textures as conceptual knowledge ensures that children are better able to use their five senses to identify, name, and discriminate between various object attributes, characteristics, and qualities at a young age.

The Bracken concept list includes conceptual knowledge across each of the five senses, except taste. Within the remaining four senses, however, the Bracken concepts comprehensively include knowledge of materials (e.g., cloth, wood), material attributes (e.g., wet, dry), material textures (e.g., rough, smooth, sharp), states of matter (e.g., liquid, solid, gas), temperature (e.g., hot, cold, boiling), sound (e.g., loud, quiet), and appearance (e.g., shiny, bright, clear, dull, dark, light).

## Quantity

Quantitative knowledge in early childhood is part of, yet distinct from, students' understanding of numbers and counting. Knowledge of numbers and counting provides the foundation for much of the quantitative understanding that follows, but not always so. For example, it is obvious that virtually all young children have acquired the concept of more before they can identify numbers or count.

Quantitative concepts, then, represent the understanding of such conditions as part/whole (e.g., whole, part, piece), relative quantity (e.g., lots, few, many, nothing, none, every), volume (e.g., full, empty), comparatives (e.g., more than, less than), multiples (e.g., double, pair, couple, triple, dozen), fractions (e.g., half, third), currency (e.g., dime, nickel, quarter), and the use and understanding of mathematical signs (e.g., +, -, =). Quantitative concepts provide young children with language that allows them to talk about numbers and counting in ways that communicate and generalize knowledge beyond the number of the objects being measured, weighed, counted, divided, distributed, or otherwise treated mathematically.

## Time/Sequence

Because life progresses temporally, from birth to death, from morning to night, from breakfast to dinner, from new to old, from yesterday to tomorrow, young students quickly attend to the temporal patterns in their lives, even if they have not acquired the language to describe those patterns. In the domain of time/sequence, there is the obvious mathematical/quantitative nature of seriation (e.g., first, second, third) and frequency (e.g., once, twice) that also must be considered.

Knowledge of time and sequence, however, is more than just a quantitative component. Time and sequence also deal with students' knowledge and awareness of natural events (e.g., morning, daytime, night), temporal order of events (e.g., starting, before, after, over, finished), temporal absolutes (e.g., never, always), scheduling (e.g., early, late, next, arriving, leaving), speed (e.g., fast, slow), relative age (e.g., new, old, young, old), and descriptive temporal nuances (e.g., nearly, just, quit, waiting).

All of the previously mentioned time/sequence related concepts are found on the Bracken concept list.

## Conclusions

The collective developmental and educational literature and the efforts of individual researchers have identified a comprehensive and unified combination of foundational knowledge that young children should know in order to ensure that all children possess a common knowledge base before entering advanced grades. This foundational knowledge is necessary to ensure that students have the language and understanding to learn about, talk about, and ask about content they learn in social studies, science, language arts, art, mathematics, and so on. This complete list of content and concepts constitute an extremely important foundation of knowledge. If all young children possessed a thorough understanding of the basic concepts subsumed by these overarching categories of content that describe and comprise this universe of basic knowledge, all students would start their formal educations on a much more even footing. The knowledge base included in the list of Bracken concepts and the instructional principles provides parents and teachers a real, nonrhetorical, practical, and proven guide for placing a solid, common, and important foundation under all young students.

# Appendix D
# Materials List

| Lesson | Materials Needed |
|---|---|
| Lesson 1: What Is a Scientist? | • Lab coat for teacher<br>• One lab coat (white adult T-shirt or dress shirt) for each student<br>• Beaker<br>• Microscope or magnifying glass<br>• Prepared charts for students, PowerPoint slides, or transparencies of Handout 1A (Defining Scientists) and 1B (What Scientists Do: The Wheel of Scientific Investigation and Reasoning)<br>• Poster of the Wheel of Scientific Investigation and Reasoning<br>• Marker<br>• One piece of chart paper<br>• Student log books<br>• *What Is a Scientist?* by Barbara Lehn |
| Lesson 2: What Is Change? | • Lab coat for teacher<br>• One lab coat (white adult T-shirt or dress shirt) for each student<br>• Enlarged picture of the teacher as a baby or young child<br>• Charts created using Handouts 2A (Things That Change) and 2B (Change Rules or Generalizations)<br>• Two large sticky notes for each pair of students<br>• Pencils<br>• Chart paper with heading Things That Don't Change<br>• Copy of Handout 2C (Change Is Everywhere) for each student |
| Lesson 3: What Scientists Do— Observe, Question, Learn More | • Lab coat for teacher<br>• One lab coat (white adult T-shirt or dress shirt) for each student<br>• Chart or slide of Handout 1B from Lesson 1<br>• Chart paper, slide, or sentence strip with the question "Why did the shadow change?"<br>• Flashlight or lamp<br>• Tennis ball<br>• Chart paper<br>• Student log books |
| Lesson 4: What Is a Shadow? | • Lab coat for teacher<br>• One lab coat (white adult T-shirt or dress shirt) for each student<br>• Chart or slides of Handouts 1B, 4A (Learning More About Shadows), 4B (Definition of Shadow), and 4C (My Observation of Shadows)<br>• Copies of Handout 4C, one for each student, or two pieces of plain paper for younger students<br>• Flashlight<br>• Stick of modeling clay or can of playdough<br>• New pencil<br>• Dark room<br>• *Light: What Is a Shadow?* by Jim Pipe (optional)<br>• *What Is a Shadow? Projects About Light* by Jackie Holderness (optional) |

| Lesson | Materials Needed |
|---|---|
| Lesson 5: What Scientists Do— Experiment, Create Meaning, Tell Others | • Lab coat for teacher<br>• One lab coat (white adult T-shirt or dress shirt) for each student<br>• Charts or slides of Handouts 1B, 5A (Definition of Hypothesis), 5B (Using a Question to Form a Hypothesis), 5C (Steps for Shadow Experiment), and 5D (Shadow Experiment Data)<br>• Copies of Handout 5E (Science Investigation Badges)<br>• Student work using Handout 4C<br>• Chart paper<br>• Flashlight or lamp without a shade<br>• Yardstick<br>• Masking tape<br>• Tennis ball<br>• Pencil or marker<br>• Student log books |
| Lesson 6: Shed a Little Light on Me | • Lab coat for teacher<br>• One lab coat (white adult T-shirt or dress shirt) for each student<br>• Charts or slides of Handouts 1B and 6A (Light Sources Chart)<br>• Slide or copies of Handout 6B (Shadows Concept Map; one for each student)<br>• *Young Thomas Edison* by Michael Dooling<br>• Student log books |
| Lesson 7: The Difference in Day and Night | • Lab coat for teacher<br>• One lab coat (white adult T-shirt or dress shirt) for each student<br>• Charts or slides of Handouts 7A (Comparing Day and Night), 7B (Definition of Rotation), and 7C (Sunrise and Sunset Chart)<br>• Toy car<br>• One ball/globe for each pair of students<br>• One flashlight for each pair of students<br>• One piece of drawing paper for each student<br>• Stickers<br>• Markers and/or crayons<br>• Bulletin board with the title "Look at Us During Sunrise, Noon, Dusk, and Midnight," with four labels for each time of day<br>• *Day and Night* by Anita Ganeri<br>• Student log books<br>• Internet access (optional) |
| Lesson 8: Me and My Shadow | • Lab coat for teacher<br>• One lab coat (white adult T-shirt or dress shirt) for each student<br>• Charts or slides of Handouts 1B, 8A (Shadow Predictions), and 8B (Shadow Investigation Question)<br>• Slide or copies of Handout 8C (Shadow Concept Map)<br>• Copies of Handout 8A, one per student<br>• *What Makes a Shadow?* by Clyde Robert Bulla<br>• Student log books<br>• Movie, *Peter Pan* |
| Lesson 9: Watching Shadows Grow | • Lab coat for teacher<br>• One lab coat (white adult T-shirt or dress shirt) for each student<br>• Charts or slides of Handouts 1B, 5A, 5E, 8B, 9A (Steps for Morning, Noon, and Afternoon Shadow Experiment), and 9B (Watching Shadows Grow Data Table)<br>• Badges made from Handout 5E<br>• Markers<br>• White butcher paper<br>• One tape measure per pair of students<br>• One piece of colored chalk per pair of students<br>• Three sticky notes per pair of students |

| Lesson | Materials Needed |
|---|---|
| Lesson 10: Temperatures in Sun and Shade | • Lab coat for teacher<br>• One lab coat (white adult T-shirt or dress shirt) for each student<br>• Charts or slides previously created of Handouts 1B, 4A, and 5A<br>• Charts or slides of Handouts 10A (Investigation Question for Temperature Experiment) and 10D (Sun and Shade Temperature Experiment Findings)<br>• Copies of Handouts 10B (Sun and Shade Temperature Experiment) and 10C (Sun and Shade Temperature Experiment Data Table), one per student<br>• Slide or copies of Handout 10F (Changing Shadows Concept Map)<br>• Badges made from Handout 5E<br>• Two thermometers for each group of 3–4 students<br>• Sunny day<br>• Shadow created by a large tree or building<br>• Student log books<br>• Copies of Handout 10E (Temperatures in the Sun and Shade Sample Graph; optional) |
| Lesson 11: The Greenhouse Effect | • Lab coat for teacher<br>• One lab coat (white adult T-shirt or dress shirt) for each student<br>• Chart or slide previously created of Handout 1B<br>• Slide or copies of Handout 11A (Sunlight Concept Map; one per student)<br>• Slide of Handout 11B (Diagram of the Greenhouse Effect)<br>• Copies of Handout 11C (Temperature in a Jar Experiment Data Table; one for each group of 3–4 students)<br>• Two thermometers for each group of 3–4 students<br>• One glass jar for each group of 3–4 students<br>• Sunny area to perform the experiment<br>• Picture of a greenhouse (optional)<br>• *A True Book: The Ozone Layer* by Rhonda Lucas Donald (optional)<br>• *Environmental Issues* posters by McDonald Publishing (optional) |
| Lesson 12: It's Getting Hot Down Here! | • Lab coat for teacher<br>• One lab coat (white adult T-shirt or dress shirt) for each student<br>• Charts or slides of Handouts 12A (Definition of Global Warming), 12B (Things We Can Do to Reduce Global Warming), and 12C (Conservation Concept Map)<br>• One silhouette of the teacher<br>• One piece of 12" x 18" white construction paper for each student<br>• One piece of plain chart paper for each group of 3–4 students<br>• One shadeless lamp or a large flashlight<br>• Masking tape<br>• Markers |
| Lesson 13: Shining With Shadows | • Lab coat for teacher<br>• One lab coat (white adult T-shirt or dress shirt) for each student<br>• Shadow Figure Templates (Handouts 13A)<br>• Directions for Creating Shadow Figures (Handout 13B)<br>• Copies of Handout 13C (What We Learned From *How the Sun Makes Our Day*; one per pair of students)<br>• One badge for each student created from Handout 13D (Official Sun and Shadow Investigator Badge)<br>• Stage or large space that can be darkened and has a large wall space<br>• One or two bright spotlights |

# References

Bracken, B. A. (1984). *Bracken Basic Concept Scale.* San Antonio, TX: Harcourt Assessments.

Bracken, B. A. (1986). Incidence of basic concepts in the directions of five commonly used American tests of intelligence. *School Psychology International, 7,* 1–10.

Bracken, B. A. (1987). *Bracken Concept Development Program.* San Antonio, TX: Harcourt Assessments.

Bracken, B. A. (1988). Rate and sequence of positive and negative pole concept acquisition. *Language, Speech, and Hearing Services in the Schools, 19,* 410–417.

Bracken, B. A. (1996). Clinical applications of a multidimensional, context-dependent model of self-concept. In B. A. Bracken (Ed.), *Handbook of self concept: Developmental, social, and clinical considerations* (pp. 463–505). New York, NY: John Wiley and Sons.

Bracken, B. A. (1998a). Basic concept acquisition and assessment: A celebration of our world's many dimensions. *Clinicians' Forum, 8*(2), 1, 7.

Bracken, B. A. (1998b). *Bracken Basic Concept Scale—Revised.* San Antonio, TX: Harcourt Assessments.

Bracken, B. A. (2006a). *Bracken Basic Concept Scale—Receptive Third Edition.* San Antonio, TX: Harcourt Assessments.

Bracken, B. A. (2006b). *Bracken Expressive.* San Antonio, TX: Harcourt Assessments.

Bracken, B. A., Barona, A., Bauermeister, J. J., Howell, K. K., Poggioli, L., & Puente, A. (1990). Multinational validation of the Bracken Basic Concept Scale. *Journal of School Psychology, 28,* 325–341.

Bracken, B. A., & Brown, E. F. (2008). Early identification of high-ability students: Clinical assessment of behavior. *Journal for the Education of the Gifted, 31,* 403–426.

Bracken, B. A., & Cato, L. A. (1986). Rate of conceptual development among deaf preschool and primary children as compared to a matched group of non-hearing impaired children. *Psychology in the Schools, 23,* 95–99.

Bracken, B. A., & Fouad, N. (1987). Spanish translation and validation of the Bracken Basic Concept Scale. *School Psychology Review, 16,* 94–102.

Breen, M. J. (1985). Concurrent validity of the Bracken Basic Concept Scale, *Journal of Psychoeducational Assessment, 3,* 37–44.

Bulla, C. R. (1994). *What makes a shadow?* New York, NY: HarperCollins.

Center for Science, Mathematics, and Engineering Education. (1996). *National science education standards.* Washington, DC: National Academy Press.

Cummings, J. A., & Nelson, B. R. (1980). Basic concepts in oral directions of group achievement tests. *The Journal of Educational Research, 50,* 159–261.

Donald, R. L. (2001). *Air pollution.* New York, NY: Scholastic.

Donald, R. L. (2001). *The ozone layer.* New York, NY: Scholastic.

Dooling, M. (2005). *Young Thomas Edison.* New York, NY: Holiday House.

Flanagan, D. P., Alfonso, V. C., Kaminer, T., & Rader, D. E. (1995). Incidence of basic concepts in the directions of new and recently revised American intelligence tests for preschool children. *School Psychology International, 16,* 345–364.

Frayer, D. A., Frederick, W. C., & Klausmeier, H. J. (1969). *A schema for testing the level of concept mastery.* Working Paper from the Wisconsin Research and Development Center for Cognitive Learning, The University of Wisconsin.

Ganeri, A. (2004). *Day and night. Nature's patterns.* Chicago, IL: Heinemann Library.

Holderness, J. (2002). *What is a shadow? Projects about light.* Brookfield, CT: Copper Beech Books.

Howell, K. K., & Bracken, B. A. (1992). Clinical utility of the Bracken Basic Concept Scale as a preschool intellectual screener: Comparison with the Stanford-Binet for Black children. *Journal of Clinical Child Psychology, 21,* 255–261.

Kaufman, A. S. (1978). The importance of basic concepts in the individual assessment of preschool children. *Journal of School Psychology, 16,* 208–211.

Lehn, B. (1999). *What is a scientist?* Brookfield, CT: The Millbrook Press.

McIntosh, D. E., Brown, M. L., & Ross, S. L. (1995). Relationship between the Bracken Basic Concept Scale and Differential Ability Scales with an at-risk sample of preschoolers. *Psychological Reports, 76,* 219–224.

McIntosh, D. E., Wayland, S. J., Gridley, B., & Barnes, L. L. B. (1995). Relationship between the Bracken Basic Concept Scale and the Differential Ability Scales with a preschool sample. *Journal of Psychoeducational Assessment, 13,* 39–48.

Novak, J., & Gowin, B. D. (1984). *Learning how to learn.* New York, NY: Cambridge University Press.

Panter, J. E. (2000). Validity of the Bracken Basic Concept Scale—Revised for predicting performance on the Metropolitan Readiness Test—Sixth Edition. *Journal of Psychoeducational Assessment, 18,* 104–110.

Panter, J. E., & Bracken, B. A. (2000). Promoting school readiness. In K. M. Minke & G. G. Bear (Eds.), *Preventing school problems—Promoting school success: Strategies and programs that work* (pp. 101–142). Bethesda, MD: NASP.

Panter, J. E., & Bracken, B. A. (in press). Validity of the Bracken School Readiness Assessment for predicting first grade readiness. *Psychology in the Schools.*

Pipe, J. (2006). *Light: What is a shadow?* Mankato, MN: Stargazer Books.

Rhyner, P. M., & Bracken, B. A. (1988). Concurrent validity of the Bracken Basic Concept Scale with language and intelligence measures. *Journal of Communication Disorders, 21,* 479–489.

Rutherford, F. J., & Ahlgren, A. (1989). *Science for all Americans.* New York, NY: American Association for the Advancement of Science.

Scholastic. (2007). *Scholastic children's dictionary.* New York, NY: Author.

Stebbins, M. S., & McIntosh, D. E. (1996). Decision-making utility of the Bracken Basic Concept Scale in identifying at-risk preschoolers. *School Psychology International, 17,* 293–303.

Sterner, A. G., & McCallum, R. S. (1988). Relationship of the Gesell Developmental Exam and the Bracken Basic Concept Scale to academic achievement. *Journal of School Psychology, 26,* 297–300.

Taba, H. (1962). *Curriculum development: Theory and practice.* New York, NY: Harcourt, Brace.

VanTassel-Baska, J. (1986). Effective curriculum and instructional models for talented students. *Gifted Child Quarterly, 30,* 164–169.

VanTassel-Baska, J., & Little, C. (Eds.). (2003). *Content-based curriculum for gifted learners.* Waco, TX: Prufrock Press.

Wilson, P. (2004). A preliminary investigation of an early intervention program: Examining the intervention effectiveness of the Bracken Concept Development Program and the Bracken Basic Concept Scale—Revised with Head Start students. *Psychology in the Schools, 41,* 301–311.

Zoom. (n.d.). *Shadow animals.* Retrieved from http://pbskids.org/zoom/activities/do/shadowanimals.html